Adult Bible Studies
Winter 2021–2022 • Vol. 30, No. 2

Teacher

To the Teacher 1
Why Wait? 14
The Spiritual Practice of Continuous Prayer 15
Hymns of Praise 48
The Spiritual Practice of Singing 59
Questions We Ask of the Bible 71
How to Look Past What's Right in Front of Us 82
The Tefillin, the Phylactery, and the Mezuzah 104
The Spiritual Practice of Testimony 114
More About Disciple-Making 144

ENGAGE
Unit 1	**Wait for It**		2
1	December 5	A Long Wait	3
2	December 12	Mary's Pondering	17
3	December 19	Waiting for Prophecy to Be Fulfilled	28
4	December 26	Jesus Is Waiting	38
Unit 2	**Wonder**		49
5	January 2	In Awe of God's Creation	50
6	January 9	Coming Into God's Presence	61
7	January 16	The Transfiguration	73
8	January 23	Beholding God's Glory	84
9	January 30	Joining the Choir of Angels	93
Unit 3	**Show and Tell**		103
10	February 6	The Greatest Commandments	105
11	February 13	Making God's Light Visible	116
12	February 20	Informing, Transforming Faith	125
13	February 27	The Great Commission	135

Editorial and Design Team
Jan Turrentine, Editor
Tonya Williams, Production Editor
Keitha Vincent, Designer

Administrative Team
Rev. Brian K. Milford,
 President and Publisher
Marjorie M. Pon, Associate Publisher and Editor,
 Church School Publications

ADULT BIBLE STUDIES TEACHER (ISSN 1059-9118). An official resource for The United Methodist Church approved by the General Board of Discipleship and published quarterly by Cokesbury, The United Methodist Publishing House, 2222 Rosa L. Parks Blvd., Nashville, Tennessee 37228. Copyright © 2021 by Cokesbury. Send address changes to ADULT BIBLE STUDIES TEACHER, 2222 Rosa L. Parks Blvd., Nashville, Tennessee 37228.

To order copies of this publication, call toll free: **800-672-1789**. FAX your order to **800-445-8189**. Telecommunication Device for the Deaf/Telex Telephone: **800-227-4091**. Automated order system is available after office hours, or order through Cokesbury.com. Use your Cokesbury account, American Express, Visa, Discover, or Mastercard.

For permission to reproduce any material in this publication, call 615-749-6268, or write to Permissions Office, 2222 Rosa L. Parks Blvd., Nashville, Tennessee 37228.

Scripture quotations in this publication, unless otherwise indicated, are from the Common English Bible, copyright 2011. Used by permission. All rights reserved. Scripture quotations taken from THE HOLY BIBLE, NEW INTERNATIONAL VERSION®, NIV® Copyright © 1973, 1978, 1984, 2011 by Biblica, Inc.™ are used by permission of Zondervan. All rights reserved worldwide. New Revised Standard Version of the Bible, copyright 1989, Division of Christian Education of the National Council of the Churches of Christ in the United States of America. Used by permission. All rights reserved. Scripture quotations from THE MESSAGE. Copyright © by Eugene H. Peterson 1993, 1994, 1995, 1996, 2000, 2001, 2002. Used by permission of NavPress Publishing Group. Scriptures quotations taken from the New American Standard Bible®, Copyright © 1960, 1962, 1963, 1968, 1971, 1972, 1973, 1975, 1977, 1995 by The Lockman Foundation. Used by permission (www.Lockman.org). Revised Standard Version of the Bible, copyright 1952 (Second edition, 1971) by the Division of Christian Education of the National Council of the Churches of Christ in the United States of America. Used by permission. All rights reserved. Scripture quotations are taken from the Holy Bible, New Living Translation, copyright © 1996. Used by permission of Tyndale House Publishers, Inc., Wheaton, Illinois 60189. All rights reserved. Scripture quotations marked CSB have been taken from the Christian Standard Bible®, Copyright © 2017 by Holman Bible Publishers. Used by permission. Christian Standard Bible® and CSB® are federally registered trademarks of Holman Bible Publishers. Scripture taken from the Modern English Version. Copyright © 2014 by Military Bible Association. Used by permission. All rights reserved. Scripture taken from the Good News Translation in Today's English Version–Second Edition Copyright © 1992 by American Bible Society. Used by Permission.

ADULT BIBLE STUDIES is available to **readers with visual challenges** through BookShare.org. To use BookShare.org, persons must have certified disabilities and must become members of the site. Churches can purchase memberships on behalf of their member(s) who need the service. There is a small one-time setup fee, plus a modest annual membership fee. At the website, files are converted to computerized audio for download to CD or iPod, as well as to other audio devices (such as DAISY format). Braille is also available, as are other options. Once individuals have a membership, they have access to thousands of titles in addition to *ABS*. Live-narrated audio for persons with certified disabilities is available from AUDIOBOOK MINISTRIES at http://www.audiobookministries.org/.

Photo Credit: Shutterstock

Meet the Writer
Taylor Mills is a United Methodist pastor originally from Raleigh, North Carolina. He received a degree in communication from Appalachian State University and a master of divinity degree from Duke Divinity School. He has led churches in Williamston, Raleigh, and Durham, North Carolina. Currently, he is the pastor of Ann Street United Methodist Church in Beaufort, North Carolina.

His wife, Betsy, works in the school system; and together they try to keep up with their two teenage daughters.

Cokesbury

To the Teacher

A few years ago, Nashville was fortunate to host Violins of Hope, a collection of violins, violas, and cellos owned and played by Jewish people before and during World War II. Unlike some of the musicians who played them, these instruments survived the horrors of the Holocaust and its gas chambers and were salvaged and lovingly restored. Canadian composer Jaap Nico Hamburger believes the instruments give "a voice . . . to musicians who showed resilience, dared to hope, and defied the odds by creating art in a place where art did not live."[1]

A work colleague, a classically trained violinist, was among a small group of musicians chosen to play one of the instruments in some local performances. At both performances I attended, with great care he removed the violin from its case and held it up. When he turned it around, most of us audibly gasped, unprepared for the beautiful mother-of-pearl inlay on the backside. But that strong response was overshadowed when he began to play the instrument, knowing as we did the story behind it and its original owner. It was mesmerizing, a holy moment.

Theologian N. T. Wright said, "The present world is good, but broken and in any case incomplete; art of all kinds enables us to understand that paradox in its many dimensions. But the present world is also designed for something which has not yet happened. It is like a violin waiting to be played: beautiful to look at, graceful to hold—and yet if you'd never heard one in the hands of a musician, you wouldn't believe the new dimensions of beauty yet to be revealed. Perhaps art can show something of that, can glimpse the future possibilities pregnant within the present time."[2]

Hope of future possibilities had grown dim for God's people during the roughly 400-year period between the time of the prophet Malachi and the appearance of John the Baptist. God offered no prophetic word during this time, yet God was at work, changing Israel's political, religious, and social landscape in preparation for the promised Messiah. God's people—indeed the whole world—were waiting for something that had not yet happened. And they had waited for a long time.

As it was when John the Baptist burst onto the scene, our world is still "good but broken and incomplete." We who are part of God's kingdom are, incredibly, partners with God in mending the broken pieces and restoring the incomplete to wholeness.

Like the Jewish musicians who created "art where art did not live," God calls us to take hope, peace, love, joy, and the presence of Christ where they are painfully absent. We tend to want to see results right away, but we discover that, in the kingdom of God, things happen on a timetable other than our own. God, sometimes silently and undetected, is always busy preparing the landscape for redemption, renewal, and new life. When pieces fall into place in a way only God can orchestrate, the results are often breathtaking.

Our lessons this quarter, written by Gary Thompson in the student book and Taylor Mills in this teacher book, challenge us to join in God's work. But they call us, as does the season of Advent, first to wait, then respond in awe at God's close presence that goes within us, before us, beside us, and behind us.

"The Word became flesh and made his home among us" (John 1:14).

Jan Turrentine

Jan Turrentine
AdultBibleStudies@umpublishing.org

[1] From *classicfm.com/discover-music/instruments/violin/violins-of-hope-endured-atrocities-vital-story-holocaust/*.
[2] From *Simply Christian: Why Christianity Makes Sense*, by N. T. Wright (*goodreads.com*).

Unit 1: Introduction

Wait for It

What does it mean to wait on the Lord? This is the question at the heart of Unit 1. We will learn that all our waiting began with Israel's wait for a Messiah. For many centuries, the prophets foretold a coming Savior who would redeem Israel and restore her greatness. Through exile, famine, persecution, and more, God's people looked to the fulfillment of the prophecies about a Messiah.

In Lesson 1, we get the first glimpse of the arrival of the Messiah when an angel was sent to Zechariah the priest. He and his wife, Elizabeth, had not been able to conceive a child, but that was going to change, said the angel Gabriel. The baby's name would be John, which means "God is gracious."

The thing to remember about this story during our Advent season of anticipatory waiting is that God makes us wait for a Savior by sending John the Baptist first as Jesus' herald. Even the way Luke tells the story, by interrupting it with the annunciation to Mary, we have to wait to see Zechariah and Elizabeth finally have their son.

Lesson 2 takes us closer to the heart of messianic expectation. We encounter Mary, the young woman who was engaged to Joseph but who learned she was to give birth to the Messiah—the Christ Child—and name him Jesus. We can learn a lot from Mary's example of waiting. She shows us that actively waiting does not always mean staying busy. It can also mean active contemplation. As an example, consider how Mary visited Elizabeth and they received joy and strength for their unique callings.

One of my favorite biblical stories comes in Lesson 3. Having grown up in the church, being there almost every time the doors were open, I can appreciate the characters of Simeon and Anna. They were righteous and devout Jews who spent much time in the Temple. This established their religious credentials and vouched for their character and wisdom. Their credentials were their seniority, their proximity to Temple life, and, most of all, the indwelling of the Holy Spirit.

We go from the first books of the New Testament to the last book for Lesson 4. Since Christmas Day will have come and gone by the time we take up this late-December lesson, we will need a special reminder that we are still waiting. We may not be waiting for Christ to be born in Bethlehem, but we are now waiting for Christ to return in glory. That's why Lesson 4 takes us to Revelation 3:20–4:11.

So as we come to this text as teachers, our classes might require of us extra patience! They will have just come from a joyful Christmas Day, complete with the opening of presents. Those presents give them joy, as well they should, but they can also be distractions from the true meaning of Christmas.

The good news of Revelation 3:20–4:11 is that, in Christmas, God has given us a way to celebrate with hope. God has given us a vision of the love of our Savior, who cares how we are doing in the enclaves of our hearts. He deserves our praise, and he loves us enough to visit us personally.

Throughout the lessons in Unit 1, God will remind us of the virtue of waiting patiently but also actively for the fulfillment of all of God's promises, especially in the birth of our Savior. May you and your class have a blessed Advent and Christmas!

December 5 | Lesson 1
A Long Wait

Focal Passage
Luke 1:5-25, 57-58

Background Text
Luke 1

Purpose
To recognize the importance of waiting on God's timing

Luke 1:5-25, 57-58

⁵During the rule of King Herod of Judea there was a priest named Zechariah who belonged to the priestly division of Abijah. His wife Elizabeth was a descendant of Aaron. ⁶They were both righteous before God, blameless in their observance of all the Lord's commandments and regulations. ⁷They had no children because Elizabeth was unable to become pregnant and they both were very old. ⁸One day Zechariah was serving as a priest before God because his priestly division was on duty. ⁹Following the customs of priestly service, he was chosen by lottery to go into the Lord's sanctuary and burn incense. ¹⁰All the people who gathered to worship were praying outside during this hour of incense offering. ¹¹An angel from the Lord appeared to him, standing to the right of the altar of incense. ¹²When Zechariah saw the angel, he was startled and overcome with fear.

¹³The angel said, "Don't be afraid, Zechariah. Your prayers have been heard. Your wife Elizabeth will give birth to your son and you must name him John. ¹⁴He will be a joy and delight to you, and many people will rejoice at his birth, ¹⁵for he will be great in the Lord's eyes. He must not drink wine and liquor. He will be filled with the Holy Spirit even before his birth. ¹⁶He will bring many Israelites back to the Lord their God. ¹⁷He will go forth before the Lord, equipped with the spirit and power of Elijah. He will turn the hearts of fathers back to their children, and he will turn the disobedient to

righteous patterns of thinking. He will make ready a people prepared for the Lord."

¹⁸Zechariah said to the angel, "How can I be sure of this? My wife and I are very old."

¹⁹The angel replied, "I am Gabriel. I stand in God's presence. I was sent to speak to you and to bring this good news to you. ²⁰Know this: What I have spoken will come true at the proper time. But because you didn't believe, you will remain silent, unable to speak until the day when these things happen."

²¹Meanwhile, the people were waiting for Zechariah, and they wondered why he was in the sanctuary for such a long time. ²²When he came out, he was unable to speak to them. They realized he had seen a vision in the temple, for he gestured to them and couldn't speak. ²³When he completed the days of his priestly service, he returned home. ²⁴Afterward, his wife Elizabeth became pregnant. She kept to herself for five months, saying, ²⁵"This is the Lord's doing. He has shown his favor to me by removing my disgrace among other people." . . .

⁵⁷When the time came for Elizabeth to have her child, she gave birth to a boy. ⁵⁸Her neighbors and relatives celebrated with her because they had heard that the Lord had shown her great mercy.

Key Verse: "The angel said, 'Don't be afraid, Zechariah. Your prayers have been heard. Your wife Elizabeth will give birth to your son and you must name him John'" (Luke 1:13).

Connect

Waiting is so hard to do. I get irritated if I have to wait more than five minutes on my "fast food." If a website takes longer than five seconds to load, I get impatient. When I accompany my wife while she goes shopping, I feel frustrated if it takes us more than a couple of minutes to make a decision on which brand of product to buy.

Most of us can now get almost anything we need shipped to us within two days. Seldom do we have to wait for movies to "come out on video," as we used to say. So many programs are available on-demand now. Just the very phrase *on-demand* says so much about our current situation. In so many ways, we no longer have to wait for people, products, information, or entertainment anymore.

Here in the Advent season, the church calls on us to wait and to be patient. This can be so difficult! Your worship leaders might be waiting until Christmas Eve to start singing your favorite Christmas carols, for example. Presents start collecting under Christmas trees in most homes, and people have to wait to open them. (Children are not the only ones who ponder what gifts are awaiting them.)

But all this waiting is teaching us patience. It's reminding us that some things are worth waiting for. The longer we wait, the more we anticipate. The more we anticipate, the greater our joy when the wait is over. Just as our parents told us to wait until Christmas to open gifts, so God tells us to wait until the appointed time for the divine promises to be fulfilled.

Consider how long Israel waited on God's promises to be fulfilled in a Messiah, one who saves: thousands of years! Through times of exile and oppression, they "waited patiently for the LORD" (Psalm 40:1, NRSV). Along the way, the prophets reminded them again and again to stay faithful to God because one day a deliverer would come.

With the start of Luke's Gospel in today's text, the long wait is nearly over. At the end of the long procession of prophets will come one more: John the Baptist. The occasion of his birth will also mark a promise fulfilled, a promise to his father, Zechariah, from the Lord, delivered by the angel Gabriel.

Zechariah and his wife, Elizabeth, were deeply connected to Temple life, but they had never had a child. At the time Gabriel visited Zechariah in the Temple Holy Place, they were too old to have children anymore. But like Abraham and Sarah before them, God would give them a child in their senior years. They would name him John.

The anticipation and birth of John the Baptist was a long time coming not just for Zechariah and Elizabeth, but for Israel. Luke tells the story in such a way that we hear the significance of this fulfilled promise for the couple and for the Lord's people and for all the world.

We will also pick up on similarities between Elizabeth's pregnancy and Mary's. Neither of them expected to bear a child—Elizabeth because of her advanced age; Mary because she had not yet been married. They both pondered what God had done—Elizabeth while she stayed at home for the first five months; Mary who treasured Gabriel's words "and pondered them in her heart" (Luke 2:19, NRSV). And Elizabeth and Mary would have a joyful encounter during their pregnancies (1:39-45).

You will no doubt enjoy exploring this story of divine pronouncement and fulfillment with your class. While our Advent waiting in this liturgical year has just begun, we can already see God fulfilling promises. A prophet and herald to the Messiah will be born to Zechariah and Elizabeth. Gabriel's prediction about John is coming to pass right in your very class time this Sunday: "He will be a joy and delight to you, and many people will rejoice at his birth" (verse 14).

Inspect

Luke began his "carefully ordered account" (Luke 1:3) of "the events that have been fulfilled among us" (verse 1) with an infancy narrative, not of Jesus but of John. Luke is the only Gospel writer to tell us the story of John's birth.

Luke 1:5. We are told at the outset John's birth happened during the time of Herod's rule. Luke's language is reminiscent of stories from the Old Testament times when Judah was ruled by kings. But Herod was a Roman client-king who was regarded by the Temple faithful as an outsider. Known as Herod the Great, he ruled from 37 BC to 4 BC.

Luke draws a contrast to Herod when he introduces us to Zechariah and his wife, Elizabeth. They were a priestly couple. He was a member of the priestly order of Abijah, an order that descended from Aaron. She was biologically descended from Aaron. Together they were deeply connected to Temple life.

Verse 6. Along with their religious credentials, we are given their character witness. They were "both righteous before God, blameless in their observance of all the Lord's commandments and regulations." Luke's language recalls many verses in the Pentateuch where characters such as Noah and Abraham were said to walk blamelessly before the Lord.

Add this to their ancestral purity in the priestly tradition (verse 5), and Luke has set this couple in a favorable light. We can already tell that something significant will happen in their lives.

Verse 7. Given what Luke has just told us about Zechariah and Elizabeth's faithfulness before God, the knowledge that they were unable to have children comes as a shock! Today, we know there are many reasons why a couple might not have children. But in first-century Judaism, it was expected that God would give children to an upstanding and religious couple such as Zechariah and Elizabeth. Deuteronomy 28:15, 18 states failure to follow God's Law could result in cursing of the womb. Zechariah would later admit he saw their inability to have children as a "disgrace" (Luke 1:25).

But this priestly couple joined other famous couples in Israel's history who were childless at one time. Like Abraham and Sarah (Genesis 18:11), Zechariah and Elizabeth were deemed too old. Samson (Judges 13:2-24) and Samuel (1 Samuel 1:2-28) were born to women who were thought unable to have children. Genesis 25:21 indicates Rebekah was unable to have children until the Lord was moved by Isaac's prayer.

Luke gives us no basis on which to assume Zechariah and Elizabeth were unable to have children because of any disobedience. Instead, Luke creates empathy in the reader and anticipation this couple might be blessed with an unexpected child like their significant ancestors. He also foreshadows Mary's unexpected pregnancy.

Verse 8. Having introduced Zechariah and Elizabeth, Luke now starts telling their story.

He begins with Zechariah, who was tending to his semiannual priestly duties. The priests of Aaron were divided into 24 divisions, each given a turn in priestly service for one week twice in the year. No doubt a pious man such as Zechariah felt honored to attend to the burnt incense during his turn (Luke 1:9).

Verse 9. Zechariah was chosen by lot from among his division to go into the Lord's sanctuary and burn incense. This further implies God had appointed him for a special task. He was physically and symbolically set apart from the people who were "praying outside" (verse 10). The altar of incense was in the Holy Place, neither outside nor all the way in the Holy of Holies. So Zechariah was as close as he could get to the presence of the Lord for his station. Many priests might never experience this honor.

Verse 10. The faithful worshipers were gathered outside to pray as Zechariah went to the altar of incense on their behalf. Isaiah 56:7 says the Temple is a "house of prayer for all peoples." Luke returned to this sentiment in Luke 18:8-14; 19:46; 24:53.

Incense was usually offered twice a day, once in the morning and once in the afternoon or evening (Exodus 30:7-8). Most commentators believe the event Luke recorded took place during the latter time.

Verse 11. Zechariah was probably accompanied by a few other priests who assisted him during the burning of incense. He may have been alone, however, when an angel of the Lord appeared to him. When the people wondered what took him so long (verse 21), no other priest who might have seen the angel gave any explanation.

The angel appeared at the right side of the altar of incense, culturally considered the favored side. Though the angel is not yet named in the story, there are some parallels between this story and the time Gabriel appeared to Daniel (Daniel 9): the time of the evening sacrifice, connected with prayer, the fear of the Lord, and the visionary being rendered mute.

Verse 12. The setting of the angel's appearance is important. This is the locus of Israel's interface with the Most High God connecting heaven and earth. Zechariah was receiving a rare epiphany. His fearful response is to be expected given the context. In Luke 1:29, we read that Mary was "confused" by Gabriel's words, but here Zechariah is "startled and overcome with fear."

Verse 13. Perhaps sensing fear, the angel said, "Don't be afraid," and called Zechariah by name. An angel said the same thing to Mary (verse 30) and to the shepherds (2:10). When these words are used in Luke and Acts, they communicate reassurance and the certainty of God's care, not judgment.

Indeed, Zechariah should have taken heart because his prayers had been heard. An angelic response to a prayer is something most people never get. Not only that, but the angel brought a birth announcement! Zechariah and Elizabeth would have a son.

Luke never actually tells us Zechariah was praying for a son. Perhaps he was praying for a biological son, or perhaps he was praying for a Messiah to deliver Israel. In either event, we will soon see their son was set aside for a divine purpose.

The angel declared the new baby would be named John. The naming of an announced child carries forward from Old Testament tradition into Luke's Gospel. *John* means "God is gracious." This name will come into play again in the last part of the story of Zechariah and Elizabeth when they both insist that the boy's name shall be John (1:57-64).

Verses 14-15. The remainder of the angel's proclamation in verses 14-17 is a list of effects John would have on his parents, his community, and Israel. Each prediction begins with "He will." John will bring delight to his parents, to "many people," and to the Lord (verse 14). In this way, the angel tied together Zechariah and Elizabeth's need for a son with Israel's need for restoration.

Since John was set aside for a special purpose, the angel added a dietary restriction. He was not to drink wine or liquor, perhaps even prenatally, which would echo the instructions given to Samson's mother (Judges 13:7).

Complete abstinence from alcohol was an ascetic behavior that was somewhat unusual in the ancient world. But instead of spirits, John was to be "filled with the Holy Spirit" even before birth (Luke 1:15). The prenatal indwelling of the Holy Spirit in him would be on exhibit when his mother (who would also be filled with the Holy Spirit) encountered Mary and the unborn Jesus (verse 41).

Verses 16-17. The angel's "he will" predictions continued. In these two verses, we see God's redemptive work in Israel in miniature. John will "bring many Israelites back to the Lord their God" like the prophets of old (verse 16). Note that he will bring many, not all. God's ministry through John would not be well received by everyone (Matthew 14:1-12; Mark 6:14-29; Luke 9:7-9).

Just as John took up the mantle of those who came before, he also prepared the people for the One who was to come to redeem Israel. "He will go before the Lord," the angel declared, "with the spirit and power of Elijah" (Luke 1:17).

Luke borrowed from Malachi 4:6, when the angel said John "will turn the hearts of fathers back to their children" (Luke 1:17). This is an interesting idiom because we might expect it to say instead he would turn the hearts of the children back to their fathers. But the positive emphasis on children continues in Luke's Gospel (9:46-48; 18:15-17). In a parallel sense, John would "turn the disobedient to righteous patterns of thinking" (1:17).

John's purpose is clearly stated at the end of verse 17: to ready a people for the Lord's coming. Luke was prefiguring Jesus, even if he has not yet mentioned the Messiah. For now, the emphasis is on how Israel's period of waiting is drawing to an end. God is about to act.

Verse 18. The seeming impossibility of the angel's message was not lost on Zechariah. Luke has already told us they were too old (verse 7). Now, Zechariah states it, too. His words are reminiscent of Genesis 18:11-12, when Abraham questioned how he and Sarah could have a child in their old age.

Verse 19. The trustworthiness of the message is in the trustworthiness of the messenger. The as-yet unnamed angel was none other than Gabriel, the one who stands in the Lord's presence. He is known from Daniel 8–9 as the one in whom God trusts divine mysteries. Zechariah could trust him for sure!

Verse 20. Gabriel made a proclamation to address Zechariah's doubt: "Know this: What I have spoken will come true at the proper time." But Zechariah had already expressed doubt for which there would have to be a consequence.

Zechariah would have to remain silent until everything in the prophecy was fulfilled, including the naming of the child (verses 59-64). Though his silence was inconvenient, it was not merely a curse. It was also a sign and a guarantee of God's promise that would be seen by the people when Zechariah emerged and gestured he could not speak (verse 22).

Verse 21. The scene changes from the altar of incense in the Holy Place to the outside world of the Temple area where the people were praying (verse 10). In this way, Luke reminds us the promise made to Zechariah was not just for him and Elizabeth. It was for Israel and the whole world.

But why were they waiting outside? They didn't know Zechariah would come out having seen a vision. They were waiting because as the main officiating priest, it was Zechariah's duty to come back out and say a blessing over the people.

Verse 22. Zechariah's muteness would now become a sign to all the people. From his gestures (which must have been creative), they would derive two things: (1) He could not speak, and (2) he had a vision in the Temple. The content of the vision was not articulated. Neither is there evidence Zechariah wrote anything about it for the people as he would do when John was named (verse 63).

Verse 23. As a dutiful priest, Zechariah did not take sick leave after his vision. He remained at the Temple performing his appointed duties. One can imagine the discussion among the priests and the people about what Zechariah must have experienced and his inability to speak.

But when the days of his priestly service were finished, Zechariah returned home. Luke then shifts the setting of the story from the Temple to Zechariah and Elizabeth's domestic life. The reader is now waiting to see the fulfillment of Gabriel's pronouncement.

Verse 24. Elizabeth's impossible pregnancy was the first sign the angel's promise would come true. But this might not have been revealed to the people yet because she kept it to herself for five months. The implication is after the five months, her pregnancy became obvious. In a way, her seclusion was a parallel to Zechariah's inability to speak. Both of them were bearers of a holy mystery.

Verse 25. Elizabeth's reaction to her pregnancy was not like Zechariah's reaction to the angel's prediction. Elizabeth gave praise to the Lord. To be fair, however, Elizabeth did not experience the fright of an angelic appearance.

Elizabeth's words are briefer than Zechariah's prophecy (verses 67-79), but we might expect that from Zechariah after he had been mute for nine months. (And this writer knows how much priests and preachers love to talk! Readers might be reminded of the wonderment of Sarah (Genesis 21:1) and Rachel (Genesis 30:23) when they, too, discovered they would have children.

In Elizabeth's words, we also have an indication her childless situation was perceived as a disgrace. This might also explain why she waited five months: so she could come out of "disgrace" and reveal "the Lord's doing" (verse 25).

Verse 57. Our focal passage picks up with verses 57-58. At this point, the angel Gabriel has made another visitation. But this one was to a virgin named Mary to announce she would conceive and bear a son who would be named Jesus. Also, Mary had gone to visit Elizabeth at which point John leapt in his mother's womb.

In verse 57, Mary has returned home, and the time came for Elizabeth to give birth to her child. Luke's word choice implies this was the fulfillment of an awaited prophecy. It also looks ahead to the language in Luke 2:6-7 in which "the time came for Mary to have her baby" and "she gave birth to her firstborn child, a son."

Verse 58. The archangel promised there would be rejoicing at the birth of this child (1:14), and so there was. Not only had the Lord removed Elizabeth's "disgrace" (verse 25), but also "her neighbors and relatives celebrated with her" (verse 58). We can presume they were happy for at least two reasons: (1) She was having a child, and (2) the favor of God was upon her.

Remember, we do not know that they had heard the content of the angel's prophecy, at least not entirely through Zechariah. Only later (verses 65-66) will they begin to pick up on the deeper dimensions of John's birth, saying, "What then will this child be?"

Nearly all of the prophecy has been fulfilled by verse 58. Zechariah and Elizabeth have had a child, a boy, and now all that remains to fulfill the angel's proclamation is for him to be named John.

Reflect

If you have the *Adult Bible Studies* DVD, plan when you will show the segment related to this lesson.

There are so many ways to capture the interest of your class members in today's text. For one thing, it's appropriate for the season of Advent. Everyone is getting excited for the celebration of Jesus' birth. They can easily transfer that excitement to John's birth, too. This can come through the endearing way in which Elizabeth and Mary were pregnant at the same time. Maybe you or someone in the class can remember a time when two of the women in a family were pregnant at the same time.

Another point of contact can be the story of Zechariah. The muting of this priest is interesting to imagine. As a preacher and writer myself, I like words. I like to talk. And sometimes it is said of preachers we must be paid per word! Can you imagine your preacher being struck mute for nine months? (Let the jokes ensue!)

There are other interesting ways to enter this text with your class. You could go on a "scavenger hunt" in the focal passage for connections to Old Testament accounts. These would certainly include the parallels to the story of Abraham and Sarah's promised child. Additionally, John the Baptist is often considered the last of the Old Testament prophets, even though we meet him in the New Testament. You can find other parallels in "Inspect."

However you come at this account of angelic pronouncement, do come around to the theme of waiting. As I said in "Connect," we have a hard time waiting. We're not used to it anymore. There has never been a time when we've had such quick access to information, entertainment, and people. But here comes Advent, calling on us to wait for the birth of the Messiah.

To approach the theme of waiting, call attention to the illustration of the century plant in the student book. Ask if anyone has had a plant like this and what their experiences were with waiting for it to bloom. Then ask: *How do you do with waiting? What makes waiting difficult for you?*

Certainly waiting is something everyone can identify with. Hear their stories of waiting. Many stories will be about waiting for products and services. Someone might mention a more profound waiting such as a long period of trying to have a child. If this happens, be sensitive and guide the conversation carefully.

Any time we talk about having children, we should remember the subject is personal. Odds are there is someone in your class, man or woman, who has desired to have children but couldn't for some reason. They might not identify themselves as such because the discussion can quickly and inadvertently become painful for them. Avoid words such as *barren* that might have stigma attached. Substitute with the technical term *infertile* or *childless*.

Refrain from giving unsolicited advice on fertility or adoption. Those who have had trouble conceiving have likely heard it all before. Though we will read how Elizabeth referred to her "disgrace," we shall contextualize that to her time and place. You can explain that the ancients connected the birth of children to God's favor.

Call attention to the information about Advent in the student book, and highlight key points there. After initial forays into the topic of waiting, read the Focal Passage, and begin discussing it. After the first reading, ask: *What parts of this story had you forgotten since the last time you heard it? What parts stand out to you?*

It's helpful to let the reading "breathe," to not dive right in to explain everything. As you listen to class members, make special note of what they say with regards to waiting. Then guide them to look for the themes of waiting in the text. *Who waited?* (*Zechariah and Elizabeth had been waiting for a child. The people waited outside for Zechariah to come out. Elizabeth waited five months before going out in public. Indeed, all of Israel had been waiting for a Messiah to be born.*)

Say: *When we think about it, Israel waited thousands of years for the Messiah to be born who would deliver them from their oppressors. Our daily waiting for goods and services is so miniscule in comparison.*

After you make this point, return to the text, reread selected verses again, and look for practical applications. For example, consider a comparison between how Zechariah and Elizabeth responded to the news from Gabriel. Zechariah and Elizabeth were deeply ingrained in Temple life. Luke tells us during the reign of Herod, it came time for Zechariah to perform his duties in the Temple.

Zechariah experienced the supernatural visitation of the archangel while he was by the altar of incense. Make use of the information in "Inspect" to explain why this setting was so significant. You might also point out the importance of Gabriel who appeared in the account of Daniel and who would soon make a pronouncement to Mary.

Ask: *How did Zechariah react to the angel's announcement?* (*He was fearful, and he was puzzled how this could be, given their advanced age.*) The angel silenced him for doubting the prophecy. He would not be able to speak again until the baby boy was born and named John. You might compare that to how Mary reacted when Gabriel told her she would bear a son.

An interesting sidebar: The ancient church father Origen pondered the significance of Zechariah's gestures to the people when he was unable to speak. "What does this mean? Zechariah's silence is the silence of prophets in the people of Israel." In other words, Zechariah's silence can be compared to how the people waited and wondered if God would ever speak through the coming of a promised deliverer.

Next, ask: *How did Elizabeth react?* (*Elizabeth was not the direct recipient of the pronouncement. Presumably, she had to interpret Zechariah's gestures as the people at the Temple did. But she no doubt understood she became pregnant!*)

Elizabeth stayed secluded for the first five months of her pregnancy, perhaps foreshadowing how Mary pondered the angel's message in her heart. Elizabeth also went on to share in joy with Mary when they met.

Ask: *How do we wait patiently for God's promises to be fulfilled? How do we react when they come to pass?*

This might be the key question for us all. We are about to see the prophecies be fulfilled in Jesus' birth. *All around us, God is keeping promises from Scripture, but how do we react? Do we take the Lord's word (whether through an angel, the Bible, or the Spirit)? Do we question the veracity of the message or the messenger?*

Review the poem "Zechariah's Annunciation" by Pamela Lee Cranston, and share it with the class (*articles.faithwriters.com/reprint-article-details.php?article=18326*).

Call attention to the information about the spiritual practice of praying without ceasing and the suggestion of *Lectio Divina* in the student book. Encourage class members to select a phrase or a verse from this week's focal passage to use in developing this practice this week.

Close with pthe prayer from the student book: **Dear God, thank you for the gift of Christmas, the coming of your Son and our Savior. Thank you for loving us, forgiving us, empowering us, and calling us to make a difference in your world. Help us to more deeply connect with you in this season of Advent; in Jesus' name we pray. Amen.**

[1] From *Luke: Ancient Christian Commentary On Scripture*, by Arthur Just Jr. (Intervarsity Press, 2003); page 10.
[2] From "Zechariah's Annunciation," by Pamela Lee Cranston, *Anglican Theological Review*, Volume 86, Number 2 (Spring 2004); pages 317–318.

Why Wait?

In Advent, while we work our way through the lessons in Unit 1, we are reminded again and again of the importance of waiting. Elizabeth waited to be pregnant (Lesson 1). Mary waited to deliver the Christ Child (Lesson 2). Simeon and Anna waited all their lives to see the Messiah (Lesson 3).

In our worship services this time of year, our ministers and musicians often make us wait before we sing our beloved Christmas carols. They tell us waiting is good for us. "It's Advent," they say. But everywhere around us, it already seems to be Christmas. And by the time it is actually Christmas on the liturgical calendar, it feels as if there is no time to sing all our favorite carols.

So why is waiting so important to the Christian life? If God is good and wants the best for us, why does God make us wait? Is God treating us like children, telling us not to look under the Christmas tree yet, as if that will make us appreciate our presents even more?

Perhaps we are told to wait because God knows us better than we know ourselves. God knows what is best for our spirits. And over the centuries, those who have listened to God the closest have told us we need to wait.

You are not surprised to be told we are a hurried people, but do you also realize we are a hungry people? We are hungrier than we realize. Our affluent culture makes us believe our spirits are well-fed, but we are malnourished. We can see this in our anxiety and listlessness.

But waiting is a way we can fast from constantly being busy and fed. When we wait to be fed, we are fasting. This can be a literal physical fasting; or it can be a fasting from something intangible such as amusement, luxury, or self-satisfaction.

So when we can't sing a Christmas carol yet or we can't open a present yet, we are reminded of our longing for God. We are reminded our life with God is a diet of spiritual nourishment. Advent comes along and, not unlike Lent, calls us to fast.

Reknowned theologian Dietrich Bonhoeffer put it this way: "Celebrating Advent means being able to wait. Waiting is an art that our impatient age has forgotten. It wants to break open the ripe fruit when it has hardly finished planting the shoot.

"But all too often greedy eyes are only deceived; the fruit that seemed so precious is still green on the inside, and disrespectful hands ungratefully toss aside what has so disappointed them."[1]

May this season of Advent be one in which you and I learn to wait. May God remind us how dependent we are on God's nourishment. It won't last forever, thank the Lord! But let it last awhile.

[1] From *God Is in the Manger*, by Dietrich Bonhoeffer (*goodreads*).

The Spiritual Practice of Continuous Prayer

Prayer, of course, is a fundamental spiritual practice, but what does it mean to "pray without ceasing"? The admonition comes from Paul in his letter to the church at Thessalonica. In closing, he wrote, "Rejoice always, pray without ceasing, give thanks in all circumstances; for this is the will of God in Christ Jesus for you" (1 Thessalonians 5:16-18, NRSV).

How can we possibly pray all the time, especially when we consider all of the other things Scripture tells us we are supposed to do? Feed the hungry. Help the poor. Visit those who are sick and in prison. Be salt and light. Teach. Baptize. Make disciples. Meet regularly with other Christian believers. Encourage one another in the faith. Worship. Serve. And love. Love without reservations. Love without limits. Love extravagantly. Love others as Jesus loves us.

How, exactly, are we supposed to "pray without ceasing" if we are busy doing all of these things, or even a few of them? And what about our jobs, our families, our responsibilities at home? Pray without ceasing? Rather than see this as a guilt-inducing command we can never achieve, think of it instead as God's gracious invitation to live in an even closer relationship with God.

It's not that complicated, but it is difficult to practice. At its basic level, to pray without ceasing is to be constantly aware of God's presence with us and constantly submissive to God's will and guidance in our lives. In a world as noisy and distracting as ours, that's quite a challenge. And it's not something we can call up quickly or turn on as we would a light. Like other spiritual practices, it is a posture we must work to cultivate.

Part of what it means is none of these other good things we are called to do are as effective and meaningful unless prayer precedes, surrounds, and follows them. It means we approach each one with the assurance and the awareness God is with us; God has, in fact, gone before us, preparing the way. It means we don't just forge ahead and expect God to bless the good things we do. It means we acknowledge we need God before we ever begin to do anything and that God works with us and through us as we do these good things.

But what about those times when we are not busy, moving from place to place and person to person? What about those times when, in the stillness and quiet, worries and anxiety overwhelm us? Then, especially then, we should "pray without ceasing." In expressing our doubts, fears, and concerns, we can also acknowledge we, by ourselves, are not enough to handle them. We need God. We need to acknowledge our dependence on God. We are not enough. But God always is. When we sit with God in prayer with our worries, doubts, and anxieties, we realize just how great God is. God is enough.

As you lead your class in studying and applying Scripture, also lead them to greater depths in prayer, in the awareness of God's constant presence and faithfulness. If you and they need ideas for infusing your days with prayer, consider these:

- Write reminders on sticky notes, and attach these to things you see first thing in the morning, as well as others you see throughout the day: the coffeemaker, your computer screen, the television, the doorframe.
- Set alarms on your phone, and stop to pray when they sound.
- Pray as you walk, run, or engage in other solo physical exercises.
- Pray as you read the newspaper or online news articles.
- Use everyday sights and sounds as reminders to pray. When you hear or see a school bus, pray for children, teachers, administrators, and parents. When you hear or see an ambulance or a police officer, pray for first-responders and those they serve. When you see a tree, flower, or garden, pray for those who grow and prepare our food. Pray for those who do not have enough to eat and for those whose diets lack the essential vitamins and nutrients necessary for growth and thriving.
- When you are alone and the house seems unbearably quiet, pray for people who are lonely, afraid, and full of doubts.
- When you are in a crowded store or mall, pray that people can learn how to live peacefully together.
- When you work in your kitchen or you are doing laundry, thank God for modern conveniences.
- When you go to the bank or pay your bills, pray for those who struggle financially. Pray for those who have lost jobs. Pray that we who have enough will be generous toward those who do not.

You get the idea. You can think of other audible and visible cues in your everyday experiences that can remind you to "pray without ceasing."

"Don't be anxious about anything; rather, bring up all of your requests to God in your prayers and petitions, along with giving thanks. Then the peace of God that exceeds all understanding will keep your hearts and minds safe in Christ Jesus" (Philippians 4:6-7).

December 12 | Lesson 2
Mary's Pondering

Focal Passage
Luke 1:26-38, 46-55

Background Text
Luke 1

Purpose
To allow Mary's simple faith to inspire us

Luke 1:26-38

²⁶When Elizabeth was six months pregnant, God sent the angel Gabriel to Nazareth, a city in Galilee, ²⁷to a virgin who was engaged to a man named Joseph, a descendant of David's house. The virgin's name was Mary. ²⁸When the angel came to her, he said, "Rejoice, favored one! The Lord is with you!" ²⁹She was confused by these words and wondered what kind of greeting this might be. ³⁰The angel said, "Don't be afraid, Mary. God is honoring you. ³¹Look! You will conceive and give birth to a son, and you will name him Jesus. ³²He will be great and he will be called the Son of the Most High. The Lord God will give him the throne of David his father. ³³He will rule over Jacob's house forever, and there will be no end to his kingdom."

³⁴Then Mary said to the angel, "How will this happen since I haven't had sexual relations with a man?"

³⁵The angel replied, "The Holy Spirit will come over you and the power of the Most High will overshadow you. Therefore, the one who is to be born will be holy. He will be called God's Son. ³⁶Look, even in her old age, your relative Elizabeth has conceived a son. This woman who was labeled 'unable to conceive' is now six months pregnant. ³⁷Nothing is impossible for God."

³⁸Then Mary said, "I am the Lord's servant. Let it be with me just as you have said." Then the angel left her. . . .

⁴⁶Mary said,

"With all my heart I glorify the Lord!
⁴⁷   In the depths of who I am I rejoice in God my savior.
⁴⁸ He has looked with favor on the low status of his servant.

Look! From now on, everyone will consider me highly favored
⁴⁹   because the mighty one has done great things for me.
Holy is his name.
⁵⁰   He shows mercy to everyone,
    from one generation to the next,
    who honors him as God.
⁵¹He has shown strength with his arm.
    He has scattered those with arrogant thoughts and proud inclinations.
⁵²   He has pulled the powerful down from their thrones
    and lifted up the lowly.
⁵³He has filled the hungry with good things
  and sent the rich away empty-handed.
⁵⁴He has come to the aid of his servant Israel,
    remembering his mercy,
⁵⁵   just as he promised to our ancestors,
    to Abraham and to Abraham's descendants forever."

Key Verse: "Then Mary said, 'I am the Lord's servant. Let it be with me just as you have said.' Then the angel left her" (Luke 1:38).

Connect

Try to think of your 12-, 13-, or 14-year-old self. What were your interests? What were you into? Being a child of the 1980s, I remember my preteen thoughts were about playing with my friends and playing computer games. The girls I knew were playing with their friends and trying makeup for the first time.

It's mind-boggling for us now to think a girl of that age could be engaged to be married as Mary was back in her time. But life expectancy was much shorter then, and the agrarian lifestyle required young people to take on many family responsibilities. We know from developmental psychology that teenagers are still learning about themselves and the world around them. They have not yet gained the wisdom and perspective of an adult.

Mary was young physically but also psychologically and emotionally. So it is all the more amazing she could ponder the otherworldly announcement from the angel Gabriel that she would bring forth the Messiah! She exhibited remarkable emotional and spiritual maturity for such a young woman!

As we will see, she did not push back on the prospect that she would bear the Christ Child. Rather, she pondered it all in her heart and accepted the angel's word, saying, "I am the Lord's servant. Let it be with me just as you have said" (Luke 1:38).

Mary's faithfulness and obedience challenge us to ask, Where are we obedient to the will of God? When we receive a call from the

Lord, do we push back, or do we ponder it and accept it?

At first, it may seem ridiculous to compare God's call on our lives to the call on Mary's life. We are not Mary. But consider what God called Mary to do: to bear the Lord within her and bring him forth to the world.

Mary did so physically, but aren't we called to do the same thing figuratively and spiritually? Aren't we called to carry the presence of Jesus within our hearts and thus bring his presence forth in the world? Of course, we are! That's something to ponder for sure!

Eastern Christianity has a special title for Mary: the Greek word *Theotokos*. It means "God-bearer." How appropriate! Mary bore the presence of God in the person of Jesus. She is an example to us of how to carry Christ into the world with faithfulness and obedience.

Just as Mary initially pondered this strange announcement from Gabriel, she later praised God for it, too. She went to see her relative Elizabeth (verses 39-45) who said to her, "God has blessed you above all women, and he has blessed the child you carry" (verse 42). The baby John the Baptist even leapt inside Elizabeth's womb when Mary came near.

The two pregnant women shared a joyous visit. One might imagine they even bonded by comparing and commiserating over the side effects of being pregnant. But there was another layer to their reunion: They were both specially blessed by God. As Luke added, "Elizabeth was filled with the Holy Spirit" during Mary's visit (verse 41).

Upon their exchange of greetings and blessings, Mary broke into song! Her song is part of the background text for this lesson, verses 46-55. Where at first Mary pondered, now she praised.

As you will read in "Inspect," Mary's song was not just about Mary. It was about all God was doing for Israel and the whole world by bringing forth the long-awaited Messiah. Mary declared Jesus' birth would have political, economic, and cosmic significance. The birth of Jesus would turn the world upside down.

Mary's song in verses 46-55 demonstrates how deeply she pondered what God was up to. She exhibited an extraordinary insight into what Jesus' birth meant, a level of insight even Jesus' own disciples didn't begin to reach until after Jesus' resurrection.

All of this makes Mary's story so compelling: her pondering and praising, her extraordinary insight. We are so blessed Luke brings us Mary's story so we, too, might seek to be faithful and obedient as God-bearers in the world!

Inspect

Our Focal Passage is the story of the annunciation to Mary and her reaction to the news. The verses that follow, which we will also unpack, include Mary's song of praise over her blessedness.

Luke 1:26. Luke narrated this verse in such a way as to connect it to the preceding story. We are told when Elizabeth finished her second trimester, "God sent the angel Gabriel to Nazareth, a city in Galilee" (Luke 1:26). It's the same angel (Gabriel) with a similar message (a birth annunciation) and a different mother (Mary).

The setting is different. We might not be surprised the great angel Gabriel would be sent to a Temple priest. But Galilee was an entirely different place. It was a lesser-known agrarian community. This is consistent, however, with Jesus' humble beginnings.

Birth annunciations as reported in the Hebrew Bible generally followed a certain pattern: (1) The angel said, "Be not afraid," (2) the angel called the recipient by name, (3) the recipient was assured of God's favor, (4) the coming child's name was pronounced, and (5) the child's future purpose was revealed. We saw this pattern in the previous lesson with the announcement to Zechariah. In the following verses, we will see it with Mary.

Verse 27. Whereas Zechariah had a title and a pedigree, Mary was known only by her engagement to "Joseph, a descendant of David's house." A Jewish engagement involved two stages: (1) a contract and the exchange of a bridal price, and (2) a wedding one year later. Luke's account indicates the events in this passage happened between these two stages.

Luke does not give Mary's age, but she could have been as young as 12, 13, or 14 years old. Luke twice mentions her virginity in this verse, emphasizing not only the miracle of her pregnancy, but her ritualistic purity as the one to bear the Son of God into the world.

Verse 28. As stated above in the notes for verse 26, in most biblical annunciations, the recipient is assured they have God's favor in the third stage. But in the annunciation to Mary, the third stage comes first! Gabriel seemingly burst on the scene and suddenly announced God's favor.

Gabriel immediately called Mary "favored one"! She then received the same assurance given to the judges of Israel: "The LORD is with you" (Judges 6:12, for example). Matthew's Gospel account conveys the same assurance by means of the name *Emmanuel*, which means "God with us" (Matthew 1:23).

Verse 29. Mary was completely blindsided by her interaction with the angel and the idea that she would bear a child. We see first in verse 29 where Luke says, "She was confused by these words and wondered what kind of greeting this might be."

Keep in mind one important difference between the annunciation to Zechariah and the annunciation to Mary is that Zechariah had prayed for a child (Luke 1:13). Mary was just going about her everyday business. There's no indication she had even the first thought about having a child.

Some scholars wonder if Mary would have been familiar with a popular Hebrew folktale recorded in the Book of Tobit in which an angel appears to a bride on her wedding night and kills her bridegroom (Tobit 3:8). If she were aware of it, such a tale would have made her all the more afraid at Gabriel's appearance.

Verse 30. Now comes the "be not afraid" part of the Annunciation, and it is combined with another declaration of divine favor. It has been said of various biblical characters they have "found favor with God" (Luke 1:30, NRSV). These include the likes of Moses (Exodus 33:12, 17) and Noah (Genesis 6:8). Generally speaking, these other esteemed biblical characters received divine favor because of their righteousness before God (in whole or in part).

In contrast, Luke gives us relatively nothing about Mary's background. We are not told about her righteousness before God. Was she especially pious? Did she keep the ritual sacrifices and observances? We don't know. Mary's favor in God's sight is based solely on her role in bearing God's Son.

Verse 31. This verse is at the heart of the Annunciation. Mary was told she would (1) conceive in her womb, (2) bear a son, and (3) name him Jesus. The name came with the Child, so to speak.

The tight compression of this announcement emphasizes it was all compulsory. The only other time an annunciation was so compressed comes in Genesis 16:11, when the Lord's messenger said to Hagar, "You are now pregnant and will give birth to a son. You will name him Ishmael."

Verses 32-33. An extended and lofty description of the Child's role follows right after the announcement of his name. Five pronouncements are made about Jesus in quick succession: (1) He will be great, (2) he will be called the Son of the Most High, (3) he will have the throne of David, (4) he will rule, and (5) his kingdom will have no end.

There is no mistaking this Jesus for another great person or prophet. Every box is checked to signify he is the long-awaited Messiah. He will be more significant than his forerunner John the Baptist. He will fulfill the promises Nathan delivered to David: "I will make for you a great name," and "I will establish the throne of his kingdom forever" (2 Samuel 7:9, 13). The angel had in mind a singular eternal ruler rather than a dynasty (or house) of David's descendants.

Mary's role was presented to her as an embedded part of God's plan for Israel and the world. She was not asked to participate. It was fully assumed she would join in this divine/human partnership.

Verse 34. Mary speaks here for the first time in the narrative. Her question was, "How will this happen?" It was not the same as Zechariah's question: "How can I be sure of this?" (Luke 1:18). Mary accepted these events would happen. Zechariah wanted confirmation they would happen.

Mary and Zechariah presented their reasons, however. Mary had not "had sexual relations with a man" (verse 34). Zechariah said he and his wife were old (verse 18).

The second stage of Mary's betrothal (the wedding) had not yet taken place. Some have wondered why Mary assumed Gabriel was talking about a son that would be conceived before she had sexual relations with a man.

Gabriel did not specify when the Child would be conceived. So why didn't Mary just assume Joseph would be the father of her child, naturally conceived, at a time after the wedding? Joseph was, of course, "a descendant of David's house" (verse 27). How would Mary know the Son she was to deliver would come before she had sexual relations with a man?

Luke confidently forges ahead with the story without addressing these questions, perhaps indicating to his readers Jesus' supernatural conception was a foregone conclusion. In this way, he could use Mary's question to set up the next verse in which Gabriel would explain how the miracle would happen.

Verse 35. The angel Gabriel addressed Mary's obstetric query in a straightforward way with no hint of anger or judgment. We are meant to see Mary as a paragon of faithfulness. In fact, Luke will make sure we hear about Mary's faith in Elizabeth's declaration: "Happy is she who believed that the Lord would fulfill the promises he made to her" (verse 45). Contrast this with Gabriel's stern reaction to Zechariah's question: "Because you didn't believe, you will remain silent, unable to speak until the day when these things happen" (verse 20).

Take note of how God would conceive the Christ Child. "The Holy Spirit will come over you" (verse 35). We might be reminded of how "God's wind swept over the waters" in the Creation story of Genesis 1:2. Or we could look ahead to Luke's other book, Acts, in which Jesus promised the disciples, "The Holy Spirit has come upon you" (Acts 1:8). And Isaiah promised a spirit from on high would be poured on the people and inaugurate a time of peace (Isaiah 32:15).

Then we learn "the power of the Most High will overshadow" Mary (Luke 1:35). Such language is reminiscent of God's cloud of presence, especially Exodus 40:35, when "Moses couldn't enter the meeting tent because the cloud had settled on it."

In any event, the conception of a child by the Holy Spirit and a human woman is completely unprecedented in Hebrew Scripture. Perhaps we are meant to draw a connection to Adam as the son of God who was made, not naturally conceived. The emphasis is on the initiative of God and God's choice to bring forth a child from human stock. "The one who is to be born will be holy. He will be called God's Son" (Luke 1:35). With these words, the Child's divine purposes were revealed. This rounds out the list of the five typical parts of a biblical annunciation as outlined above, but this is no typical child!

Verse 36. Though Mary had not requested a sign, one was given to her: If Elizabeth could bear a child, Mary could be sure the promise delivered by Gabriel would come to pass for her as well. Though John the Baptist was conceived naturally when Zechariah returned from his priestly duties, he was still a miracle baby because Elizabeth "was labeled 'unable to conceive'" (verse 36). The implication is that Mary did not know Elizabeth was pregnant. This is plausible because Elizabeth remained in seclusion for five months (verse 24).

Gabriel contributes to the forward momentum of Luke's narrative by directing Mary's attention to her relative Elizabeth, who "even in her old age . . . [had] conceived a son" (verse 36). This is a setup to the next section (verses 39-45) in which Mary visited Elizabeth.

Verse 37. "Nothing is impossible for God." This verse hangs in many a home or church room as a reminder of God's omnipotence. Its context is found in the annunciation to Mary. If God can bring forth a son of a human, supernaturally conceived, then God can do absolutely anything.

These words echo the wonder of Sarah who asked, "Is anything too difficult for the Lord?" (Genesis 18:14). We can also look ahead in the Bible to Jesus' statement: "What is impossible for humans is possible for God" (Luke 18:27).

To Mary in the moment of the Annunciation, these parting words of the angel Gabriel were a promise and a declaration of divine praise. Barren women and virgins will have children if God so chooses. God calls into being what is not.

Verse 38. Luke brings us Mary's second and final response to Gabriel in which she was completely subservient to God's will. As a young woman, not as yet experienced in the way of family, she accepted an unprecedented future because she was "the Lord's servant" (verse 38). Here we see scriptural echoes of Hannah's story in which she said to Eli, "Please think well of me, your servant" (1 Samuel 1:18) before singing her song of praise (1 Samuel 2:1-10; Luke 1:46-55).

Having completed his mission, the angel Gabriel left Mary. The narrative is now free to move forward as it follows Mary's journey to visit Elizabeth and records her song of praise.

Verses 46-55. Following the story of Mary's visit to Elizabeth and the reaction of Elizabeth's baby, the narrative pauses for a song of praise from Mary. Her lyrical words are about her blessedness and the effects of the Lord's coming for all people.

Mary's song is traditionally called "the Magnificat" because that is its first word in Latin: to magnify. So some translations read, "My soul magnifies the Lord" (Luke 1:46, NRSV). In this way, her song echoes the psalms of praise that begin with praise and then elucidate the reasons for that praise (for example, Psalms 8, 33, 47, 100, 135, 136).

We can divide the Magnificat into two sections: (1) verses 46-50, in which Mary speaks to how she is personally blessed, and (2) verses 51-55, which focus on how the birth of Jesus will change the world.

Verses 46-50. The first basis for Mary's praise was that God had looked with favor on her in her lowliness. "He has looked with favor on the low status of his servant" (verse 48). We noticed Mary's low status back in verses 26-38. She was young, unknown, unmarried, and living in the backwaters of Galilee.

The second basis for Mary's praise comes in verse 49: "Because the mighty one has done great things for me." Her point was that God was doing battle with the enemies of God's people. Though she was speaking in the first person, she expressed the sentiment of all Israel.

Verses 51-55. Now the implications of the Annunciation for all people are coming into view. In each of these verses, Mary stated a reversal of fates in which the haughty are brought low and the lowly are raised up.

Mary declared God scatters the proud, brings down the powerful, and sends the rich away empty-handed. Her implication is that these proud, powerful, and rich people have opposed God's purposes for Israel in the past, but that will stop with the arrival of the Messiah!

Reflect

"Nothing is impossible for God" (Luke 1:37). This verse is blazoned across a banner that hangs in the fellowship hall of Avent Ferry United Methodist Church in Raleigh, North Carolina. It serves as a word of hope and encouragement to the congregation. All who see it are reminded God can do anything!

The verse comes from the Focal Passage for this lesson, the annunciation to Mary. It was a word of praise from God's own messenger angel Gabriel. He had just finished telling Mary she would be impregnated by the Holy Spirit to carry the Christ Child into the world!

By the grace of God, Mary accepted this radical pronouncement. She was understandably puzzled and perhaps afraid. But she did not push back. She readily accepted her role in God's salvific work, saying, "Let it be with me just as you have said" (verse 38). What remarkable faith!

This lesson will surely be enjoyable for you and your class as you come alongside Mary as her story unfolds. You will no doubt already be in the Christmas spirit, so this lesson provides you with an opportunity to thicken the plot, so to speak, of the Christmas story. It's a time to back up to the events that led up to Jesus' birth and see how the promise of God unfolded.

Meet your class members where they are by acknowledging their excitement over the coming Christmas: *We are excited to be only 13 days from Christmas! Today, we will look at how Mary received the news of the first Christmas. In her young age, she was told by the angel Gabriel she would be given a child by the Holy Spirit. How do you think you would react if you were in her situation?*

If you have the *Adult Bible Studies* DVD, show the segment related to this lesson at this time.

Enlist volunteers to read aloud Luke 1:26-38. Notice how this text picks up where the text for the previous lesson left off. You may want to point out similarities and differences between the annunciations to Zechariah and Mary. Especially note how Mary reacted differently than Zechariah. Mary did not resist the angel's message. She only asked how such a marvelous thing would take place. Ultimately, she accepted the news with great faith, especially for someone so young.

As mentioned in "Connect," we could consider this story to be her pondering. She took it all in and considered what kind of strange word this was from Gabriel. As Luke explained, "She was confused by these words and wondered what kind of greeting this might be" (Luke 1:29). Similarly, when the shepherds visited the Holy Family, we read, "Mary treasured all these words and pondered them in her heart" (2:19, NRSV). Ask: *What does it mean to ponder a word from the Lord?*

Often, when I am in a decision-making group in my church or denomination, we consider something, and then we "pray on it." For me, that has been a catch-all term to mean I pray, wait, pray some more, wait, and pray some more. I find it helpful to "sleep on it," too. We must give our spirits time to listen to the Lord, especially if God is calling us to a momentous act of faith.

Mary seems to have been an introspective young woman with a remarkable capacity to receive and follow God's call on her life. We say in the Purpose Statement for this lesson she inspires us with her simple faith. Gary Thompson states it so well in our student book: "As we reflect on this beautiful story, we can draw strength and encouragement from the simple but powerful faith of this poor, young girl. Mary's example reminds us we can trust God to keep promises and remain with us."

Use the following comments and questions from the student book to help class members further consider and apply the truths we find in this text:

- The Jews waited for many years for the coming of the Messiah. What can we learn from them as we wait for Jesus' return?

December 12, 2021 25

- The angel Gabriel assured Mary of God's presence with her.
- Do you feel God is always with you? Is there anything you might need to do to become more aware of God's presence?
- News of Mary's pregnancy and its unusual circumstances no doubt spread quickly in her little town. She was likely met with disbelief, scorn, and ridicule.
- How have you responded when you were condemned or ridiculed, even though you knew you were innocent?

The story of the annunciation to Mary is so compelling that you might run out of time in class to also consider Mary's song, Luke 1:46-55. But try to make time to guide your class through these verses as well. They form a song or hymn attributed to Mary in which she declares the magnitude of what God is doing by sending the Messiah. Just as she pondered in the Annunciation story, she praised in these verses.

The story of Mary visiting Elizabeth falls between verses 26-38 and these verses, and it ties Lesson 1 to this one. It is brief enough to include in your in-class reading for Sunday. Note that it was in the context of her visit with Elizabeth that Mary sang her song of praise.

Say: *Imagine the two pregnant mothers together. It was out of their shared joy that Mary sang her song traditionally called the Magnificat.* (See "Inspect" for an explanation of this term.) We have all seen God do something wonderful in our lives. *How do we react to God's mighty deeds? Do we remember to praise God?*

Ask a volunteer to read aloud Mary's song (Luke 1:46-55). It's not just a happy poem. It's a profound theological statement. The first part (verses 46-50) is about what God was doing through Mary. The second part (verses 51-55) is about the consequences of God's wondrous action for all people.

In the first part, we see how Mary had incredible insight for a young woman of her background! Her pondering paid off, so to speak. She saw how her life was now part of God's saving acts that were promised "to Abraham and to Abraham's descendants forever" (verse 55)

Mary rose to the call that had been placed on her life, stating, "He has looked with favor on the low status of his servant" (verse 48). God's favor in her life was not about riches or prominence. It was about her unique role in God's plan of salvation. Perhaps Elizabeth summed it up best: "Blessed is she who has believed that the Lord would fulfill his promises to her" (verse 45, NRSV)!

In the second part of her song, Mary points out how the promised Messiah will turn everything upside down throughout the world: The arrogant will be scattered, and the powerful will be pulled down; but the lowly will be lifted, and the hungry will be filled.

We've seen this kind of reversal of fates in Jesus' own teaching. The Beatitudes, for example, state the poor, hungry, and weeping people will be blessed, while woe will come upon those who are rich and laughing (6:20-26). We might also recall the reversal of fates in the story of the rich man and Lazarus (16:19-31).

Indeed, Mary was saying something bold and prophetic in her song! The young woman from the backwoods of Galilee was now empowered by God's Spirit to preach like the prophets of old. The joy of her womb became the joy for all people, especially the downtrodden.

Mary's joy is our joy, too. She can remind us Christmas is not about material gain through shopping and presents. It is about the promise for all people as it first came to her: that God "has looked with favor on the low status of his servant. Look! From now on, everyone will consider me highly favored because the mighty one has done great things for me" (1:48-49).

Ask: *How will your Christmas be different this year because of Mary's simple faith?*

Close by praying together the prayer at the end of the lesson in the student book: **Dear God, help us increase our awareness of your constant presence in our lives and to be inspired by the amazing faithfulness of the mother of Jesus; in Jesus' name we pray. Amen.**

December 19 | Lesson 3

Waiting for Prophecy to Be Fulfilled

Focal Passage
Luke 2:25-38

Background Text
Luke 2

Purpose
To remember God rewards those who act faithfully

Luke 2:25-38

²⁵A man named Simeon was in Jerusalem. He was righteous and devout. He eagerly anticipated the restoration of Israel, and the Holy Spirit rested on him. ²⁶The Holy Spirit revealed to him that he wouldn't die before he had seen the Lord's Christ. ²⁷Led by the Spirit, he went into the temple area. Meanwhile, Jesus' parents brought the child to the temple so that they could do what was customary under the Law. ²⁸Simeon took Jesus in his arms and praised God. He said,

²⁹"Now, master, let your servant go in peace according to your word,
³⁰   because my eyes have seen your salvation.
³¹You prepared this salvation in the presence of all peoples.
³²It's a light for revelation to the Gentiles and a glory for your people Israel."

³³His father and mother were amazed by what was said about him. ³⁴Simeon blessed them and said to Mary his mother, "This boy is assigned to be the cause of the falling and rising of many in Israel and to be a sign that generates opposition ³⁵so that the inner thoughts of many will be revealed. And a sword will pierce your innermost being too."

³⁶There was also a prophet, Anna the daughter of Phanuel, who belonged to the tribe of Asher. She was very old. After she married, she lived with her husband for seven years. ³⁷She was now an 84-year-old widow. She never left the temple area but worshipped God with

fasting and prayer night and day. ³⁸She approached at that very moment and began to praise God and to speak about Jesus to everyone who was looking forward to the redemption of Jerusalem.

Key Verse: "A man named Simeon was in Jerusalem. He was righteous and devout. He eagerly anticipated the restoration of Israel, and the Holy Spirit rested on him" (Luke 2:25).

Connect

Who doesn't love to see a new baby? When your coworker brings his or her new baby to the office, when you see a proud parent pushing a stroller down the sidewalk, when a baby is brought to worship for baptism, it seems as if everyone loves to see a new baby.

Mary and Joseph brought their new baby Jesus to the Temple "to present him to the Lord." They were also there because the time had come for Mary's "ritual cleansing, in accordance with the Law from Moses" (Luke 2:22). But we can imagine them being full of joy, too, as any new parent is.

It turned out their parental joy would be eclipsed by a greater power: the Holy Spirit. Luke went to great lengths to impress upon us the Child Jesus was to be "a light for revelation to the Gentiles and a glory for your people Israel" (verse 32). For two righteous and devout Jews from the Temple, Simeon and Anna, approached the Holy Family and pronounced Jesus was the one Israel had been waiting for.

Luke tells us the credentials of these two old prophets. He wrote as much or more about their credentials as he did about what they actually said. Their credentials were their seniority, their proximity to the Temple life, and (most of all) the indwelling of the Holy Spirit (verse 27).

Perhaps you know some Simeons and Annas in your life or in your congregation. It is a blessing to see intergenerational fellowship in the church such as when a senior saint holds a new baby in the church nursery. In my home church, the same dear woman taught the four-year-old Sunday school well into her late 90s. She died at 107, having taught at least three generations of children in her class!

The Holy Family's trip to Jerusalem was primarily about Jesus, but it was also about Mary and Joseph. The way Luke tells the story, Jesus' parents experienced alternating highs and lows. For example, when they first encountered Simeon and heard what he prayed regarding Jesus, they "were amazed by what was said about him" (verse 33). But Simeon's next prophetic word was about how Jesus would be "the cause of the falling and rising of many" (verse 34).

Finally, Simeon's words cast a shadow over Mary's joy: "And a sword will pierce your innermost being too," he said (verse 35). Up and down for mother Mary!

Just as they traveled to Jerusalem in verse 22, "they returned to their hometown, Nazareth in Galilee" (verse 39). They were faithful parents, fulfilling their obligations in the civil law (verse 4) and the religious law (verse 22). We saw the same emphasis in an earlier lesson from John the Baptist's parents, Zechariah and Elizabeth.

No one could read Luke's account of Jesus' formative years and find any fault in him. His parents did everything right. Jesus' impeccable upbringing was important in the ancient world in which much was made of the sins of the fathers. Recall, for example, how Jesus' disciples encountered a blind man and asked, "Who sinned so that he was born blind, this man or his parents?" (John 9:2).

As Luke tells us at the end of our background text, "The child grew up and became strong. He was filled with wisdom, and God's favor was on him" (Luke 2:40). The story that follows is about how Jesus' parents took him to Jerusalem when he was 12 years old; but after his parents left, Jesus stayed behind, "sitting among the teachers, listening to them and putting questions to them. Everyone who heard him was amazed by his understanding and his answers" (verses 46-47).

People began to see this Jesus Child was special, something Simeon and Anna pointed out early on. As Simeon said, God has "prepared this salvation in the presence of all peoples" (verse 31).

Inspect

I've added a few verses to the beginning and end of our discussion for context. All of Chapter 2 is, in fact, good background for this lesson.

Luke 2:19. Having delivered Jesus and hosted the shepherds, Mary had a brief time in which she "treasured all these words and pondered them in her heart" (Luke 2:19, NRSV). We can see similarities between this verse and Luke 1:24, in which Elizabeth "kept to herself for five months," and Luke 2:51, in which Mary "cherished every word in her heart."

Though she must have been exhausted from childbirth (in a stable no less), Mary had not lost her contemplative spirit. Contrast her demeanor with the shepherds, who "went quickly" to find Mary, Joseph, and the Baby (verse 16), "reported what they had been told" (verse 17), and then "returned home, glorifying and praising God" (verse 20). Like Anna (from whom we will hear later in this text), the shepherds were the first evangelists in Luke.

Verses 22-23. The time came for Mary, Joseph, and Jesus to have "ritual cleansing, in accordance with the Law from Moses" (verse 22). Luke included this detail to assert that Jesus was born to religiously reliable parents. They were carrying out the actions that were normal for the birth of a firstborn son in a Jewish family: circumcision, naming, purification of his mother, presentation, and consecration.

Before her purification, Mary was not allowed to touch anything sacred or to even enter the Temple (Leviticus 12:1-8). Her purification had to happen in Jerusalem 40 days after the birth of a male child (or 80 days after the birth of a female child).

Jesus would be presented in the Temple as the firstborn of Mary and Joseph (Exodus 22:29; Nehemiah 10:36). This was also possibly an allusion to 1 Samuel 1:28, where Samuel was dedicated to the Lord.

Luke refers to what is "written in the Law of the Lord" (Luke 2:23) and probably refers to Exodus 13:12, which says, "You should set aside for the LORD whatever comes out of the womb first."

Verse 24. Also in keeping with the Law, Joseph and Mary sacrificed "a pair of turtledoves or two young pigeons." According to Leviticus 12:8, this was the alternative offering available to families who could not afford a sheep. What Luke does not mention here is that firstborn sons could also be redeemed from priestly service by the payment of "five shekels of silver" (Numbers 18:15-16).

Verse 25. As we follow the turns in Mary's story during the first days and weeks after Jesus' birth, Luke includes two blessings, one from Simeon and one from Anna. Simeon was "righteous and devout," and Anna was "an 84-year-old widow" who "never left the temple area" (Luke 2:37). Together they would further establish Jesus' religious credentials.

Luke tells us Simeon also "eagerly anticipated the restoration of Israel, and the Holy Spirit rested on him." In this way, he was similar to Zechariah, whom we met in the previous lesson: a righteous man associated with the Temple who acted under the Holy Spirit (1:5-6). Simeon's eager anticipation of the restoration of Israel mentioned here and the "looking forward to the redemption of Jerusalem" in verse 38 serve as bookends that give his story a forward-looking orientation.

Verse 26. Simeon had even received a divine revelation himself: "that he wouldn't die before he had seen the Lord's Christ." Stop and think about it: That's a significant promise he heard from God! Luke celebrated how it was coming true on this day when Simeon would greet the Christ Child.

Verse 27. This is the third verse in a row in which Luke mentions the Holy Spirit in relation to Simeon. Simeon "was in Jerusalem" (verse 25) and was inspired to go to the Temple area at the same time as the Holy Family. We presume they met in an outer area of the Temple because Mary could not go beyond the Court of Women.

Simeon's rendezvous was divinely choreographed, for it was there he encountered Jesus in the company of his parents. They brought him there "so that they could do what was customary under the Law" (verse 27). This is an echo of verses 22-23, in which the Gospel writer was more specific.

Though the Holy Spirit inspired Simeon to go to the Temple at that moment, the encounter is the result of human obedience to the divine purpose. They met in the Temple, the appointed place of human and divine interaction. This was the first stage of the gospel witness that would begin in Jerusalem and move to Judea, Samaria, and to the ends of the earth (Acts 2:8).

Verse 28. Taking Jesus in his arms, Simeon praised God. Before he gave God his "song" (verses 29-32), he instinctively knew Jesus was the one to fulfill God's promise to him (verse 26) and to Israel. Like the angelic chorus in verse 13, Simeon was filled with praise before he spoke.

Verses 29-30. Your Bible translators probably gave verses 29-32 poetic indentations on the page. This was Simeon's prayer/poem/song directed to God as he held the Child Jesus. It borrowed heavily from the vision of salvation in Isaiah 40–66.

The Latin translation of the first few words is *Nunc dimittis* ("Now you dismiss"), which has become the song's name in church tradition. It is also called the Song of Simeon or the Canticle of Simeon. It is often part of a prayer that closes the day (like vespers) in which the worshiper prays, "Let your servant go in peace" (Luke 2:29).

Simeon's prayer to depart could also be interpreted to mean he could die in peace having seen the Lord's Christ (verse 26). Or it could mean to discharge from faithful service.

In either case, Simeon could now be at peace: "Because my eyes have seen your salvation" (verse 30), by which he meant Jesus as God's instrument of salvation. His eyes had seen "a light for revelation" that would later be seen by the Gentiles and Israel (verse 32). The task of this faithful servant was complete!

Verses 31-32. What God did was not for Simeon only. It had been "prepared" as "a light for revelation to the Gentiles," "for your people Israel," and ultimately "*all* peoples" (italics added). Here, we see Luke's favorite emphasis on the outward radiating nature of the gospel message (Acts 1:8) and on how salvation is as much for the Gentiles as for the Jews (Acts 9:15; 11:15, 18, 20; 14:1; 15:9, 16-18; 18:4; 19:10, 17; 26:18, 23).

Verse 33. This is one of those special times that the narrator gives us insight into how Jesus' parents were affected by all that had happened. We have read about Mary's ponderings (Luke 2:19) and Joseph's thoughts (Matthew 1:20). We know they thoughtfully brought Jesus "to Jerusalem to present him to the Lord" (Luke 2:22).

Now we are told about their emotional state and reaction to Simeon's words. They were "amazed" (verse 33). Luke uses this term in verse 18, when everyone is amazed at what the shepherds told them.

Verses 34-35. After telling us how Jesus' parents reacted, Luke narrows the focus to

Mary, who received a pronouncement from Simeon, who shifted from prayer to dialogue. We can see a parallel between Simeon's words and the priestly blessing Eli gave to Samuel's parents (1 Samuel 2:20; Numbers 6:23).

Simeon first predicted Jesus would have two effects: (1) He would be "the cause of the falling and rising of many in Israel," and (2) he would be "a sign that generates opposition" (Luke 2:34). This opposition would lead to the revealing of "the inner thoughts of many" (verse 35). We can clearly hear the foreshadowing of Jesus' Passion in Simeon's words. Furthermore, we can hear an echo of Mary's Song when she claimed through Jesus, God "has pulled the powerful down from their thrones and lifted up the lowly" (1:52).

Last, Simeon turned his pronouncement to Mary herself: "A sword will pierce your innermost being too" (2:35). By this, he implied an emotional sword, not a spiritual sword. Readers will no doubt recall Jesus' mother looked upon her crucified Son (John 19:25). In contrast to the joy in Luke 2:29-33, the mood has now turned somber. Simeon's words must have left Mary with many questions, but those will have to go unanswered as the focus moves to an encounter with Anna.

Verses 36-37. Anna serves as a counterpart to Simeon. Both were prophetic, aged, and pious. And both of them reacted to the Boy Jesus entering the Temple. Remember, Luke was chiefly concerned with situating Jesus' birth and blessing in the story of God's salvation for Israel, then the Gentiles, and then the whole world.

Whereas Simeon was quoted, Anna was not. But like Simeon, she was introduced with a number of clauses designed to show her impeccable credentials as a person of devout faith and insight. We do not know anything else about her father, Phanuel, but we know she was from the Northern tribe of Asher.

We are told much more about her age as a signifier of her wisdom and honored place in the community. Luke noted she was old (Luke 2:36) but also added she was an "84-year-old widow" (verse 37). Some interpreters, presuming she married at 14 and understanding since she "lived with her husband for seven years" (verse 36), think she might have been 105 years old, adding the number 84 to her age of 21 when she was widowed. Because of a technicality in the Greek, some Bible translations say she was a widow to the age of 84. Suffice it to say she had lived a long life.

Anna is also meant as an example of ascetic ideal (in her cultural situation) in that she married once and then remained devoted to God, even though she had only seven years with her husband. Anna's activity in the Temple was "fasting and prayer night and day" (verse 37), never leaving the Temple area.

Verse 38. Just as Simeon arrived at the right moment to meet Jesus and his parents, so too did

Anna approach "at that very moment." This further implied the divine hand was at work behind the scenes, orchestrating these encounters.

Regardless of whether Anna heard Simeon's pronouncement, she knew what was going on, too. She recognized the child's significance, so we are told she "began to praise God and to speak about Jesus to everyone." Luke is specific about her audience, which we must assume she spoke to in subsequent days. They were "everyone who was looking forward to the redemption of Jerusalem." Presumably, this would include Simeon, who "eagerly anticipated the restoration of Israel" (verse 25). Again, Luke set these encounters in the larger framework of God's salvific work for Israel.

Verse 39. Joseph and Mary went to the Temple to fulfill their religious obligations (verses 22-23). Now "they had completed everything required by the Law of the Lord" (verse 39). Their obedience was not legalism so much as it was part of establishing Jesus' credentials as Messiah. Had his parents not done everything required of them, it would have been a blemish on Jesus' authority in the eyes of Luke's first audience. Instead, he would be raised by parents who had accepted his divine purpose.

It is interesting Luke did not mention anything about a trip to Egypt (Matthew 2:13-23) before returning to "their hometown, Nazareth in Galilee" (Luke 2:39).

Verse 40. We know relatively little about Jesus' growing-up years. Other than the forthcoming story about trips back to Jerusalem for Passover and Jesus being waylaid when he was 12, we are only given verse 40: "The child grew up and became strong. He was filled with wisdom, and God's favor was on him."

But what Luke tells us is religiously and ritualistically important: Jesus did not lose God's favor. What was said over him by everyone from Gabriel to Simeon to Anna still held true. In fact, he grew in wisdom, which will be on display in the next story (verses 40, 41-52). Verse 52 bookends these statements by reiterating "Jesus matured in wisdom and years, and in favor with God and with people."

We can find Old Testament parallels to this verse in Genesis 21:8, 20; Judges 13:24; and 1 Samuel 2:21, 26. As in those stories, Luke shows the progression of God's presence throughout Jesus' life.

Reflect

In this Advent season, our minds are already turning to the birth of the Christ Child in the manger in Bethlehem. But as any parent will tell you, the birth of the baby is just the beginning. Babies have a lot of accessories: stroller, swing, crib, bassinet, tiny clothes, and lots and lots of diapers. The first days, weeks, and months are a swirl of feedings, rockings, family visits, and little sleep.

New parents also have rituals to attend to. Grandparents, great-grandparents, aunts, uncles—everyone wants to hold the baby. There are baby's first outings: the park, the store, the church, and the office.

The whole new-baby experience is wonderfully joyous and interminably exhausting for the parents. It seems everyone wants to hold the baby! Who can blame them? Babies are precious. Most every parent has had what we call in our family a "mini-breakdown." Mommy or Daddy needs a break, sometimes together, and not every new baby outing is pleasant.

No doubt, you or those in your class will have stories of baby firsts, including first outings. Others can tell a good story about a baby baptism in church. These baby stories can serve as a way to introduce the Scripture about Jesus' presentation in the Temple.

If you have the *Adult Bible Studies* DVD, show the segment related to this lesson.

After sharing stories and watching the video, refer to the opening paragraphs of the lesson in the student book in which the writer talks about bucket lists. Use these thoughts to introduce Simeon and Anna and the one thing they wanted to do before they died.

Next, involve volunteers in reading aloud Luke 2:22-38. Then ask: **How would you describe what Mary and Joseph must have felt when approached by Simeon and Anna?** Responses may range from elated to intimidated.

Point out the family journeyed from Nazareth to the Temple in Jerusalem for two purposes: (1) to have Mary ritualistically cleansed and (2) to present Jesus to the Lord. Yes, Luke 2:22 refers to "their ritual cleansing" in the plural, but it was Mary who was deemed ritually impure after childbirth. The information about purification, ritual, and pronouncement of blessings was to convince Luke's readers Jesus had impeccable religious credentials.

Say: **Even as a child, Jesus was judged by the piousness of his parents. Do we still do that today?** Ask class members to give examples. For example, everyone has seen a well-behaved young family in church at one time or another and thought, *Those parents sure raise those children right!* Sadly, we have been known to judge some parents by the negative behaviors of their children, too. Ask: **How do you suppose Mary and Joseph felt about their Son being the subject of prophecy and speculation?**

Next, take a closer look at Simeon's prayer to God when he finally held the baby Messiah. Simeon said he could finally "go in peace" because "my eyes have seen your salvation" (verses 29, 30). In other words, Simeon could die happy, knowing he had seen the coming salvation of Israel.

The church father Origen once wrote of this passage: "This is true not only of Simeon but of the whole human race. Anyone who departs from this world, anyone who is released from prison and the house of those in chains, to go forth and reign, should take Jesus in his hands. He should enfold him with his arms and fully grasp him in his bosom. Then he will be able to go in joy where he longs to go." Ask: *Can you relate to Simeon's relief at having seen the Savior?*

Call attention to "Confirmation and Hope" in the student book, and encourage class members to discuss the questions at the end of that section.

Though Mary and Joseph were at one moment amazed (verse 33), they could have also been concerned when Simeon said to Mary, "This boy is assigned to be the cause of the falling and rising of many in Israel and to be a sign that generates opposition so that the inner thoughts of many will be revealed" (verses 34-35). In addition, take a look at what Simeon told Mary: "And a sword will pierce your innermost being too" (verse 35). It's enough to make any parent shudder.

Sometimes people say things to new parents that make them concerned: stories of when their own children got sick or hurt, warnings about what not to feed the baby, or even outright criticisms. Consider, for example, the dirty looks airplane passengers sometimes give parents of crying babies. Some upscale restaurants designate seating sections or nights of the week as child-free. Some cruises and resorts don't allow children, not to protect their safety, but to keep them unseen and unheard. Unwelcome!

Ask: *Where have you seen children and their parents made to feel unwelcome? How did it make you feel?*

The good news is that Simeon and Anna were overjoyed to meet the Christ Child. We read that Simeon was living for this moment. Anna had "never left the temple area but worshipped God with fasting and prayer night and day" anticipating this moment (verse 37). Simeon and Anna were examples to us of how to make a family feel welcome at church. Ask: *How can we make parents with babies feel welcome? (Having good nurseries and nursery workers for them is a start.)*

Church members will sometimes say, "Why should we pay nursery workers when there are no babies in our church?" Some young parents visit a church because they remember going to church when they were young. Imagine their disappointment when they arrive and must miss everything because there is no nursery worker. They must take care of their own baby in the nursery. They must wonder why they ever bothered.

It is important that a church always be completely ready for children and babies. Not only is it vital to the future of the church, it is the right thing to do. Look at how Simeon and Anna blessed Jesus and his parents by their presence in the Temple. Consider how Mary was able to live out her simple faith because she was made to feel welcome. As overwhelmed as she must have been, she "committed these things to memory and considered them carefully" (verse 19). Even as Simeon spoke of a sword, she accepted her role in Jesus' upbringing.

And "when Mary and Joseph had completed everything required by the Law of the Lord, they returned to their hometown, Nazareth in Galilee" (verse 39). This trip to Jerusalem had a beginning, a purpose, and an end. They probably returned for every Passover afterward. Luke's next story is about the Passover festival when Jesus was 12.

With or without the blessings from Simeon and Anna, "the child grew up and became strong. He was filled with wisdom, and God's favor was on him" not just because he was a good kid, but because he was the one who would restore Israel (verse 40) and bring salvation to the world.

Review briefly "Salvation for All" in the student book, and note the many scriptural references to Jesus offering salvation to everyone. But we can see from the blessings of Simeon and Anna that God's plans come to fruition in this small Child, the firstborn of Joseph and Mary. All those who have waited for the prophecies to be fulfilled will find reward for their patience and vigilance.

Remind class members Advent is a season of waiting. Ask them to think about their life of faith and their walk with Christ, and consider these questions from the lesson in the student book: *What have you had to wait for? What has come slowly for you? What did the act of waiting teach you?*

Then ask: W*here are you seeing God's promises fulfilled around you by Jesus Christ? How has the birth of the Savior given you a sense of spiritual fulfillment this year?*

Close by praying together the prayer at the end of the lesson in the student book: **Great and loving God, give us a keen awareness of your presence in our lives and help us better connect with you; in Jesus' name we pray. Amen.**

[1] From *Luke: Ancient Christian Commentary On Scripture*; page 48.

December 26 | Lesson 4
Jesus Is Waiting

Focal Passage
Revelation 3:20–4:11

Background Text
Same

Purpose
To more fully appreciate the radical nature of God's patient love

Revelation 3:20–4:11
²⁰Look! I'm standing at the door and knocking. If any hear my voice and open the door, I will come in to be with them, and will have dinner with them, and they will have dinner with me. ²¹As for those who emerge victorious, I will allow them to sit with me on my throne, just as I emerged victorious and sat down with my Father on his throne. ²²If you can hear, listen to what the Spirit is saying to the churches."

¹After this I looked and there was a door that had been opened in heaven. The first voice that I had heard, which sounded like a trumpet, said to me, "Come up here, and I will show you what must take place after this." ²At once I was in a Spirit-inspired trance and I saw a throne in heaven, and someone was seated on the throne. ³The one seated there looked like jasper and carnelian, and surrounding the throne was a rainbow that looked like an emerald. ⁴Twenty-four thrones, with twenty-four elders seated upon them, surrounded the throne. The elders were dressed in white clothing and had gold crowns on their heads. ⁵From the throne came lightning, voices, and thunder. In front of the throne were seven flaming torches, which are the seven spirits of God. ⁶Something like a glass sea, like crystal, was in front of the throne.

In the center, by the throne, were four living creatures encircling the throne. These creatures were covered with eyes on the front and on the back. ⁷The first living creature was like a lion. The second living creature was like an ox. The third living creature had a face like a human being. And the fourth living creature was like an eagle in flight. ⁸Each of the four living creatures had six wings, and each was covered all around and on the inside with eyes. They never rest day or night, but keep on saying,

"Holy, holy, holy is the Lord God Almighty,
   who was and is and is coming."

⁹Whenever the living creatures give glory, honor, and thanks to the one seated on the throne, who lives forever and always, ¹⁰the twenty-four elders fall before the one seated on the throne. They worship the one who lives forever and always. They throw down their crowns before the throne and say,

¹¹"You are worthy, our Lord and God,
   to receive glory and honor and power,
      because you created all things.
         It is by your will that they existed and were created."

Key Verse: "Look! I'm standing at the door and knocking. If any hear my voice and open the door, I will come in to be with them, and will have dinner with them, and they will have dinner with me" (Revelation 3:20).

Connect

The operative word during Advent has been *waiting*. It's what Advent is all about. We wait for the Messiah to be born in Bethlehem and to return someday to finish what he started. We are doing so much waiting for Jesus that we might not realize how much Jesus is waiting on us, too.

When we consider all that God has gone through with the human race—the fall, rebellion, disobedience, and even Jesus' crucifixion—it's amazing God continues to be so patient with us. We don't deserve it, but here is Jesus in today's text, waiting at the door of our hearts for us to open the door and let him in.

This Sunday, I hope we will more fully appreciate how patient God is with us. We're not the easiest companions for God to put up with in creation! But thanks be to God that we are shown a vision in today's text of the throne room of heaven in which Jesus will be praised by the faithful. We can take encouragement that someday God's purposes for the world will come to fulfillment.

As Gary Thompson says in the student book, "The church has been waiting for over 2,000 years, but this text reminds us Jesus stands at the door of each heart, patiently waiting, every day. He knocks because he wants us to invite him in." Jesus is far more patient than we ever are.

So as we come to today's text as teachers, our classes might require of us some extra patience! They have just come from a joyful Christmas day, complete with the opening of presents. Those presents give them joy as well they should. But they can also be distractions from the true meaning of Christmas.

Be patient with them as they adjust to a Sunday lesson from Revelation. We will want to lower their awkwardness or defensiveness about a challenging text in which Jesus comes to inspect their lives as he did the Christians in Laodicea. Ultimately, however, we will revel together in a glorious vision of heaven in which

Jesus is praised with the casting of crowns and songs such as, "Holy, holy holy" (Revelation 4:8).

May your preparation for this lesson bring you joy and encouragement as a teacher. Hopefully, you will find the complicated text satisfactorily explained below. But be patient with yourself. Remember how patient God is with you and with all of us.

God has called you to teach the Word this week! God wants you to teach the Word this week! As God said through Isaiah, "My word . . . does not return to me empty. Instead, it does what I want, and accomplishes what I intend" (Isaiah 55:11).

Inspect

The text for this lesson straddles the transition between two major parts of Revelation. The end of Revelation 3 is the end of a series of letters to seven churches (Revelation 2:1–3:22), specifically the end of the letter to the church in Laodicea. Revelation 4 is the beginning of a section on adoration in the court of heaven (4:1–5:14).

These seven letters to the seven churches are special proclamations in which Christ comes to inspect his churches and issue words of encouragement and/or warning. They are addressed to "the angel of the church in . . . " (3:14), but the expectation was that they would be read by the members of those churches. The message comes from "the Amen" (verse 14), who is Jesus Christ.

Revelation 3:14-19. The letter to the church in Laodicea is noticeably negative. It begins with a well-known saying that is often assumed to be in the Gospels: "So because you are lukewarm, and neither hot nor cold, I'm about to spit you out of my mouth" (verse 16). The Laodiceans needed to side with Jesus and stay there, says the letter. This is followed by the Amen's advice that they rely not on their own wealth, but on the "gold from me that has been purified by fire" (verse 18), the spiritual riches of following Christ.

Verse 20. Jesus described himself as a visitor knocking on the door of a household and requesting hospitality. This was a common occurrence in the ancient Near East, especially in the heat and after nightfall.

You and your class members might recall the painting *The Light of the World*, by William Holman Hunt, that hangs in many a church hall. In it, Jesus holds a lantern with one hand and prepares to knock on an overgrown, unopened door with the other hand. The artist painted no handle on the outside of the door, signifying it can only be opened from the inside. This represented the shut mind, Hunt once explained.

Apparently, Jesus also called out when he knocked because he said, "If any hear my voice" (verse 20). Though the letter is addressed to the church, the response to Christ's knock and voice calls for an individual response.

Hospitality codes of the time anticipated the visitor would be provided a meal. So Jesus would review their hospitality when, as he said, he "will have dinner with them, and they will have dinner with me" (verse 20).

Keep in mind this would have been viewed in its time as unusual behavior by a god. The

Romans and other groups in the area did not conceive of their gods and goddesses making housecalls on mortals. But Israel's God was portrayed as a seeking God. So the Christians in Laodicea should not presume they were self-sufficient in every way. Rather, they should expect Christ would call on them individually to inspect their lives.

The image of Jesus knocking on the door of the heart is useful in evangelism. But in the context of the rest of the letter to the church in Laodicea, we see Jesus had come to their door to inspect their already-Christian lifestyle by putting their hospitality to the test.

Verse 21. If the homeowner passed Jesus' test, he or she would "emerge victorious." Other versions say he or she would be "the one who conquers" (NRSV) or the one "who overcomes" (NASB). This phrase has military and athletic connotations, but here it is used to describe faithfulness. Those who remained true to their convictions despite persecution will have "conquered."

The end reward will be great for these overcomers: They will be allowed to sit with Jesus on his throne! Their victory and exaltation will follow the pattern of Christ, who also overcame persecution by his faithfulness. He referred to how he "emerged victorious and sat down with my Father on his throne" (verse 21). As Paul also promised, "if we endure, we will also reign with him" (2 Timothy 2:12, NRSV).

Verse 22. This short verse reminds us of the phrase "Hear the word of the Lord" often found in the Hebrew Bible (for example, Isaiah 1:10; Jeremiah 2:4; NRSV). It is similar to Jesus' saying, "Whoever has ears to listen should pay attention!" (Mark 4:9). In this spot, it serves, along with Revelation 2:7, as a bookend for the letters to the seven churches.

Revelation 4:1-11. Our scene shifts to the court of heaven for Revelation 4:1–5:14. John of Patmos, the recorder of the visions or revelations, was swept up in the Spirit to the door of heaven (Revelation 4:1). He beheld a vision of God ordering the course of human history. The great throne room scene was meant to encourage believers to be faithful to God, even during persecution, because God is still in control.

Verse 1. Here, we again encounter the image of a door. But this is not a continuation of the metaphor we just read about, Jesus knocking at an individual's door. This is the door to heaven! It is similar to how Ezekiel reported in his vision: "The heavens opened and I saw visions of God" (Ezekiel 1:1). The voice that commanded John to write (Revelation 1:10-11) now bade him to look at God's heavenly court.

Verse 2. John viewed himself as being in a "Spirit-inspired trance" that allowed him to see things he would not otherwise see. This was a continuation of his ecstatic state from Revelation 1:10. In this state, the Spirit would take him through phases of revelation that he might also be "shown" Babylon (17:3) and New Jerusalem (21:10).

Verse 3. In the last verse, John said, "Someone was seated on the throne" (4:2). In this verse, he describes that one's beautiful bejeweled appearance as being like jasper, carnelian, and emerald.

Where John lived, jasper referred to various precious stones ranging from green to blue or purple to rose. Carnelian was a reddish stone. Both are also used to describe the New Jerusalem in Revelation 21:11, 18-20.

John's emerald rainbow recalls other rainbows in the Bible: Genesis 9:13; Ezekiel 1:28; and Revelation 10:1, in which a rainbow was over an angel.

Verse 4. Around the throne were 24 thrones with 24 elders seated on them. The significance of the number *24* is it is a multiple of 12, a number that symbolizes the whole people of God (12 tribes of Israel, 12 apostles).

The 24 elders symbolized the future glory of the faithful. They wore white robes and gold crowns. As we will see, they joined with the four creatures to "give glory, honor, and thanks to the one seated on the throne" (verse 9), and they would later disclose the meaning of visions (4:10-11; 11:16-18).

Verse 5. The rich imagery of John's revelation continued as lightning and thunder joined voices from the throne. Biblical storms often conveyed the power of divine revelations such as those from Mount Sinai (Exodus 19:16), Ezekiel's vision (Ezekiel 1:4-14, 28), and elsewhere in Revelation (8:5; 11:19; 16:18).

John also saw seven flaming torches, which were the seven spirits of God. Again, we are reminded of Ezekiel (Ezekiel 1:12-13). Some commentators theorize these were the seven spirits in Revelation 1:4, who later become the seven eyes of the Lamb in Revelation 5:6.

Verse 6. In front of the throne, John saw a sea of glass. Keep in mind the glass of antiquity was opaque compared to glass made today. So the crystal clarity of this sea of glass was supernatural to John's eyes.

This celestial sea recalls the Creation story of Genesis 1:6-7, in which God established a dome over the earth. Above the dome were the waters of heaven and God's dwelling place.

A new element of the vision begins with the description of the "four living creatures encircling the throne." They joined the 24 elders previously mentioned. They had a central location as they encircled the throne.

The creatures would often lead the elders in worship by offering praise and prayers of petition to God (Revelation 4:9-10; 5:8-10), saying amen to the worship (5:14; 19:4), and remaining beside the throne (7:11; 14:3). Sometimes the creatures would summon powers against the earth as the seals were opened (6:1-8; 19:7).

Each creature could see all around them as they had "eyes on the front and on the back," symbolizing their watchfulness (4:6). With their six wings also covered with eyes (verse 8), they often remind readers of Ezekiel's vision of cherubim (Ezekiel 1:4-10) and Isaiah's seraphim (Isaiah 6:2).

Verse 7. Each creature was different. The first was like a lion, the second like an ox, the third like a human, and the fourth like an eagle. Again, there were similarities to Ezekiel's cherubim (Ezekiel 1:4-10), but there were differences too. For example, in Ezekiel, each creature was the same, but each had four different faces (as lion, ox, human, and eagle).

In the Christian tradition, each of the creatures is paired with a Gospel writer and often depicted holding a book. Usually, Matthew is paired with the human face because he began his Gospel with a genealogy. Mark is the lion because he began with John the Baptist roaring in the desert. The ox symbolizes Luke because he began with sacrifices offered in the Temple. Finally, John is matched with the eagle because of his Gospel's soaring opening verses.

Keep in mind, though, in the time of the writing of this revelation, the church had not yet canonized the four Gospels as we have them now. In fact, this pairing of creatures and Gospel writers was started by Irenaeus, second-century Christian theologian, as part of his argument for the inclusion of only those four Gospels in our Bible.

Verse 8. The six wings on each of the four creatures may suggest their swiftness in God's service. Remember in Ezekiel 10:16, the chariot-throne of God was carried on the wings of the cherubim.

These wings were covered with eyes. The literal translation says they had eyes "around and within" the wings, but some translators have made that less awkward: "eyes all around, even under its wings" (NIV). The visions were meant to excite the imagination.

Their continuous adoration lasted day and night. Like the angelic hosts of Isaiah 6:3, they sang, "Holy, holy, holy is the Lord God Almighty." We may think of Reginald Heber's popular 1826 hymn in which each verse begins with those words. Indeed, Heber's second verse references the golden crowns and glassy sea from before. It praises the Lord God almighty "who wert, and art, and evermore shalt be," echoing the last line of verse 8 and emphasizing God's eternal existence.

Verse 9. Continuing the emphasis on God's eternal existence, John called God the one "who lives forever and always." Since God will not cease to exist, their praise must "never rest day or night" (verse 8). This served to encourage the Christians of the time never to stop praising God, even during times of persecution.

Verse 10. Whenever the creatures praised God (which was always), "the twenty-four elders fall before the one seated on the throne." They prostrated themselves, a posture usually associated with praise in the Jerusalem Temple. The word *worship* originally connoted prostrating oneself before a deity to kiss the divine feet or the hem of a garment.

The elders were also continually casting their crowns (verse 4) before the throne, acknowledging their authority was granted to them only through God's omnipotent authority. In Roman times, it was not unusual for a vassal king to remove his crown and place it before the statue of the emperor.

Verse 11. The elders also sang, "You are worthy, our Lord and God." In John's time, the worthiness of an ancient ruler was usually based on his deeds. An accomplished ruler was worthy, but a tyrant wielded power he did not merit.

God is worthy because God "created all things." The elders addressed God directly when they said, "It is by your will that they existed and were created." The literal Greek translation is awkward: "They were and they were created."

Some translators believe John was trying to say all things always existed in God's will even before God brought them into being. But it is better to take John's awkward wording as his poetic way of saying all things depended on God for their creation.

Reflect

It's the day after Christmas. Our floors at home are probably still covered in balls of wadded up wrapping paper. Parents with children in the home are probably tired as they come to church this morning. This being a holiday weekend, several of your class members may still be out of town visiting family. And you might have a few visitors who come with some of your class members.

It's safe to assume people will be in a good mood. The Christmas spirit will be strong. It is a joyful time. There may be extra fellowship and chatter as class members gather and share their Christmas stories.

So how do you corral them into looking into a text from Revelation, considered by many to be a complicated and daunting book to study? As in other teaching opportunities, it's best to meet them where they are by letting them enjoy sharing their special Christmas stories.

Then, when it is time to get started, you could say something like this: *I'm so happy we had a wonderful Christmas Day yesterday. It sounds as if we had lots of fun celebrating Jesus' birth. Our text today is about a celebration, too: a worshipful celebration John saw in heaven.*

I recommend familiarizing yourself with the first part of "Inspect," in which I point out the context of the last part of Revelation 3 (the letter to the church in Laodicea) and the beginning of Revelation 4 (the vision of heaven). You will likely need to return to this delineation to help the class navigate John's imaginative writing.

If you have the *Adult Bible Studies* DVD, show the segment related to this lesson.

Explain to the class how you will be reading about two doors: (1) the door of the heart in Revelation 3:20 and (2) the door of heaven mentioned in Revelation 4:1.

Ask a volunteer to read aloud Revelation 3:14-22 and Revelation 4:1.

Say: *In Revelation 3 and 4, John (the writer of Revelation) uses a door to symbolize the point of connection between us and Jesus. Jesus is knocking on a door, and John is peering through a door.* Then ask: *What does the image of a door convey to you about how we interact with God?*

It is possible someone will point out the door of the heart (Revelation 3) symbolizes that Jesus does not force his way into our hearts. He stands at the door and knocks. This would be a good opportunity to recall the Holman Hunt painting mentioned in the note on Revelation 3:20 above.

If possible, print from an online source an image of the painting to show the class. Or, if your church has a replica of this painting displayed somewhere, arrange to borrow it to show them. Point out the artist's decision not to put a door handle on the outside of the heart's door.

Point out in Revelation 3:20, Jesus stands at the door and knocks. He also calls out. Ask for volunteers to talk about a time when they felt Jesus knocking on their heart's door.

Hopefully, you will have some who will respond. Be patient, and allow class members time to reflect so someone might respond aloud. (Even a little awkward silence is good at getting discussion going.) Think ahead of time of your own response to this question, too, and be prepared to respond first if you need to.

When did you feel Jesus knocking on the door of your heart? It doesn't have to be the first time a person ever heard Jesus' knock. Many of us grew up in the faith and can't point to one first time we heard Jesus' knock. It could be a time later in life when Jesus came to "inspect" our hearts.

Point out the whole letter to the church in Laodicea (Revelation 3:14-22) is about how Jesus comes to inspect the church. The part about the heart's door is about how Jesus comes to inspect our own hearts, especially by way of our hospitality (verses 20-22). He wants to know if we have been listening to him and following his teachings.

Supplement your comments and those of class members by adding information about Laodicea from the introductory paragraphs to this lesson in the student book. Ask a volunteer to read aloud the paragraph in that introductory section beginning, "Just as God had not given up on the Laodicean Christians, God has not given up on us."

Stress that Jesus knocks on our heart's door not just to enter our hearts but, as we see in this text, to inspect our hearts and our lives. Ask: **What do you think he is looking for?**

Be sure to leave enough time in your discussion to look at Revelation 4. Ask a volunteer to read aloud Revelation 4:1-11. You will probably need to remind the group that this is apocalyptic literature.

The word *apokalypsis* is Greek and means "discover" or "revelation" (hence the title of the book). This kind of writing usually consists of visions and dreams that uncover secrets of the divine world. (Look for a great description of apocalyptic literature from Gary Thompson in this lesson in the student book.)

We don't see a lot of new apocalyptic literature in the West these days, but it was common in John's time. It was a time in which Christians were being persecuted. So a lot of the symbolism in Revelation is about the struggle of the faithful against the powers and principalities of their world at the time. It is also future-focused, another characteristic of apocalyptic literature. The idea is the visions will give hope to the Christians under persecution as they see that someday God will win! Their troubles will not last forever.

Lead the class to examine Revelation 4:1-11 verse by verse. Acknowledge the imagery and writing style can seem intimidating. Your purpose is not to decode the writing as if you were trying to figure out exactly when these things will happen. What you want to do is to simply enrich their understanding of what John is trying to say.

Use the commentary in "Inspect" to interpret the symbols to them. You may want to draw a diagram for them at the front of the classroom. For example, you could draw a doorway off to the side through which John and an angel are peering into heaven. Draw a throne in the center where Jesus is seated. Then put 24 smaller thrones in a circle around him (but leave room to add the torches and creatures near the middle). On each of the 24 thrones sits an elder.

Then draw the seven flaming torches in front of the throne. And then by the throne, draw the four creatures: one like a lion, one like an ox, another like a human, and the last like an eagle.

(This drawing does not need to be a work of art! In fact, you and the class could have fun making it. Perhaps you could ask for different volunteers to come up and draw the different elements of the scene as you describe them.)

Stress what we have here is an otherworldly scene. This is how John saw the court of heaven where God is praised. Ask: *What do you think of such an image? What do you like about it?*

Allow time for class members to take in all of the elements of the scene and then give initial reactions. Assure them they don't need to feel they must understand it all or interpret it in detail. You might need to remind them it is a poetic vision. Like a lot of things that are too beautiful to describe, John was reaching for the best words he could find to paint a picture.

Then ask: *What do you think the purpose of the vision was? How would it have helped the early Christians under persecution to imagine this scene as you are doing today?*

Next, key in on the vision's purpose: to give hope and encouragement to Christians. Tie this chapter of Revelation to the end of Chapter 3 by saying: *The Christians in Laodicea were under a close inspection by Jesus. In some ways they were found wanting. But what would the vision in Revelation 4 have meant to them? What do you think their reaction was when they read it?*

I like to imagine the Christians of Laodicea being encouraged even as they were being inspected. Isn't that how it is to live as a follower of Jesus? When we read Jesus' more difficult teachings (turn the other cheek; let the dead bury the dead; sell all your possessions, and give the money to the poor) we feel we are under inspection. Jesus comes to visit our hearts and see how we're doing in our discipleship.

But then he also gives us comfort saying, "Come to me, all you who are weary and burdened, and I will give you rest. . . . For my yoke is easy and my burden is light" (Matthew 11:28, 30). And he gives us (through John of Patmos) a vision of heaven in which God is in charge. All of this brings us peace and encouragement. We can persevere in our discipleship because we realize this is all God's work in the end, and God will emerge victorious over evil.

Close your class time by circling back to Advent and Christmas. Say: *We've just come through Advent in which we anticipate Jesus' birth in Bethlehem long ago as well as his return to someday set things right. Now we're in the 12 days of Christmastide celebrating the fulfillment of God's promise of a Messiah.*

Jesus is knocking on your heart's door today. He wants to come in and see your discipleship for himself. What will he find? How will this Christmas be different?

And be encouraged yourself as a teacher! You've taken the class through a portion of Revelation on the day after Christmas! That's no small feat.

End on a high note. Say: *This Christmas, let us celebrate with hope because God has given us a vision of eternity in which the one who comes into our hearts will include us in the multitudes who sing his praises! We join the heavenly hosts to praise Jesus forever and ever! It will be far greater than even our favorite Christmases!*

Close by praying together the prayer at the end of the lesson in the student book: **Loving God, thank you for your presence in our lives and your desire to live in our hearts and minds. Help us deepen our relationship with you, to hear your call upon our lives, to learn of your ways, and to do your will; in Jesus' name we pray. Amen.**

[1] *The United Methodist Hymnal*, 64.

Hymns of Praise

Throughout the lessons in Unit 2, we will be enthralled with awe-inspiring visions, poetry, and imagery that will fill our hearts with praise. And the heart of all praise in the Bible comes from the Psalms. The Psalms were (and are) the Hebrew hymnal, lyrical verses that cover the gamut of emotions. Some of the greatest words of praise in the Bible—or anywhere—are found there.

So let's take a look at praise as a genre, especially lyrical praise. Today, we have hymns of praise to God in nearly every language spoken. We have centuries of them, from Gregorian chants to contemporary praise and worship songs and everything in between. What, then, makes a good praise hymn or song? Why are we drawn to some special ones?

Keep in mind our preferences are often affected by our upbringing. We love the songs we grew up singing. Everybody does, and it's always been that way.

But would you believe that at one point people thought "Amazing Grace" was a newfangled, contemporary song? We can even find old sermons in which preachers railed against the new tunes such as "Holy, Holy Holy"!

It's amazing to consider the Psalms themselves, as well as some of the medieval chants, have been around a lot longer than the more contemporary songs. God's people should always be singing a new song because God is always doing a new thing. But there's something to be said for the staying power of the praise music that is centuries old.

The United Methodist Hymnal includes an excerpt from *John Wesley's Select Hymns of 1761* called "Directions for Singing." John Wesley wanted to make sure the people called Methodists knew how to sing songs of praise "lustily and with a good courage." He wrote, "Beware of singing as if you were half dead, or half asleep, but lift up your voice with strength. Be no more afraid of your voice now, nor more ashamed of its being heard, than when you sung the songs of Satan."

Whatever we sing to the glory of God—whether it is an ancient psalm, a medieval chant, a Southern gospel favorite, or a contemporary praise chorus—let's sing it to God's glory!

[1] *Hymnal*; page vii.

Unit 2: Introduction

Wonder

The theme for this unit, "Wonder," reminds me of how different people react differently to surprises or to receiving presents. Perhaps you know someone who dislikes surprises. Or maybe you can think of people who get so excited they can't keep a secret.

Lesson 5 is about the awe of God's creation. When we talk creation, we usually think of Genesis 1 or 2, of course. But there are other "creation stories" (to use that term loosely) in other parts of the Bible. One is in Psalm 19:1-6. Like some other psalms, the poetry here celebrates the glory of God's creation.

When we get to Lesson 6, we still encounter poetry (as evidenced by how your Bible translation might have parts of the text indented). But this poetry is song lyrics and angelic proclamations.

Lesson 7 is by far one of the most awe-inspiring stories in all of the Bible. It is full of multisensory imagery. And we experience the story through Peter, James, and John, who themselves were filled with awe. We will be looking, of course, at the transfiguration of Jesus.

Rather than creating awe in the people by the thunder and lightning of Mount Sinai, God decided to let the divine glory come among the people by way of Moses' person. This was unprecedented in Hebrew Scripture. For Christians, it serves as a prefiguring of the way God would eventually come among us in the person of Jesus Christ.

However, the important thing to learn from Lesson 8 is we may only ever see a distant reflection of the glory of God in this life. But the good news is we don't have to be Moses to reflect God's glory, at least insofar as God shows it to us. Even from just the smallest amount of God's glory that has been revealed to us, we stand in awe.

Our journey through the Bible to look for examples of awe and wonder ends with the last book of the Bible: Revelation. The apocalyptic literature of John's Revelation lends itself to scenes of great awe. Toward the end of the book, we read about how God wins in an epic battle against Babylon and evil in general. And when God wins, the angelic hosts celebrate with singing! Their songs make up most of the content of Lesson 9.

For Lesson 9, you'll see I suggest having a class party. Who doesn't like a party? Perhaps playing a recording of the "Hallelujah Chorus" as class members walk in will generate interest. It will certainly be a fitting conclusion to our series of lessons on awe and wonder.

We have so few opportunities for awe in our lives. How wonderful it will be to journey through this unit together and be reminded of God's greatness!

January 2 | Lesson 5
In Awe of God's Creation

Focal Passage
Psalm 19:1-6

Background Text
Psalm 19

Purpose
To affirm God as the Creator and Sustainer of everything

Psalm 19:1-6
¹Heaven is declaring God's glory;
   the sky is proclaiming his handiwork.
²One day gushes the news to the next,
   and one night informs another what needs to be known.
³ Of course, there's no speech, no words—
      their voices can't be heard—
⁴   but their sound extends throughout the world;
      their words reach the ends of the earth.
God has made a tent in heaven for the sun.
⁵ The sun is like a groom
   coming out of his honeymoon suite;
   like a warrior, it thrills at running its course.
⁶ It rises in one end of the sky;
   its circuit is complete at the other.
      Nothing escapes its heat.

Key Verse: "Heaven is declaring God's glory; the sky is proclaiming his handiwork" (Psalm 19:1).

Connect

"I go to church every Sunday when I go hunting, preacher," the man told me. I had asked him why we didn't see him in our Sunday services. "I'm out there with nature, and that's church for me. I'm out there with God."

Set aside for a moment the fact that worship is not about just us and God. It's also about being together in the "two or three" or more Jesus spoke about (Matthew 18:20). Another concern I have with this man's statement that he goes to "church" in nature is he comes close to ascribing deity to nature.

What he is talking about is natural theology that bases God's existence on proof in nature. But as Christians, we have a revealed theology based on Scripture and God's self-revelation to us. If we want to know God, we don't just go outside; we go to God.

It is God who has given us Scripture such as the psalm for this lesson in which God reveals the sky speaks God's praises. It's in the first words of the psalm: "Heaven is declaring God's glory; the sky is proclaiming his handiwork" (Psalm 19:1). And then we learn day and night speak to one another in ways we cannot hear. But "one day gushes the news to the next, and one night informs another what needs to be known" (verse 2).

I'm sure the man I spoke to enjoys the beauty of creation, but I don't think he's writing inspired Scripture about it like we have in Psalm 19. We need God's Word to do that. We benefit from the poet's God-breathed words to tell us what God is like and what God does, even through the observable world.

And that's where Psalm 19:7-14 has so much to say. These verses are about "the LORD's Instruction," that is the Law, or Torah (verse 7). The psalmist extolled the virtues of God's law as it was handed down to the people of Israel. You'll find a helpful breakdown of the Hebrew Bible (or the Old Testament) books into their respective categories in the lesson corresponding to this one in the student book.

Psalm 19 has a beautiful way of affirming God as the Creator and Sustainer of everything: first, through the glory of the sky; then, through the beauty of God's law. It will bless you and your class as you read and reflect on it.

C. S. Lewis said that in his opinion, Psalm 19 was "the greatest poem in the Psalter and one of the greatest lyrics in the world."[1] Perhaps you agree, or maybe you would say another psalm is the greatest. But Lewis's praise for Psalm 19 is worth noting. And we can add our appreciation for how this psalm points to nature as a cosmic voice that sings out God's praises.

In just this one psalm, we learn that the God who separated the waters to form the sea and the sky (Genesis 1:6-8) is the same God who is our forgiving kin. The divine love that formed the cosmos comes from the same source as the divine love that redeems us from our sins, even our "unknown sin" (Psalm 19:12).

May we pray the last verse along with the psalmist:

> "Let the words of my mouth
>   and the meditations of my heart
>   be pleasing to you,
>   Lord, my rock and my redeemer" (19:14).

Inspect

This psalm of thanksgiving is a particular kind: a thanksgiving for God's Torah (or instruction, law). This is sometimes called a wisdom psalm. Among all the other psalms, it is most similar to Psalm 1 and Psalm 119, which famously says, "Thy word is a lamp unto my feet, and a light unto my path" (119:105, KJV). See also Gary Thompson's reference in the student book to other psalms such as Psalms 8 and 104, which highlight God's glory through creation.

Psalm 19 is also embedded in a series of royal psalms (18, 20–21). Royal psalms would have been of particular applicability for Israel's kings and rulers, who were to remember God is King and ruler over all.

Readers of Psalm 19 will find today's Focal Passage, verses 1-6, focuses on Creation while the rest of the psalm deals with Torah. Though we will gravitate to the first six verses in our study, we should see them in their larger context.

For example, note the sun is mentioned in verse 4. Then the effects of the sun are referenced in verses 8 ("giving light") and 11 ("your servant is enlightened"). Some scholars say in using the sun as a metaphor for God's law, the psalmist was writing an argument against the sun worship in the Assyrian religion. (See the corresponding lesson in the student book for an excellent introduction to the context in which this psalm was written and used.)

Psalm 19 instructs the faithful to appreciate God's Word and to give it priority in their lives.

Psalm 19:1. The writer began with the cosmic. In the early Jewish Creation story (Genesis 1:6-8), God separated the waters into the waters of earth (the sea) and the sky. It was understood heaven was above the sky-water "dome." This Hebrew term, which also meant "firmament," was like an upside-down bowl that sat over the ground protecting the ground below. The celestial objects moved up there on the inside of the firmament. Therefore, the psalmist was declaring here the praise of God starts in heaven and continues down through our sky to us.

How often we look up and see God's "handiwork" when we look at the sky during the day or at night. Sunrises, sunsets, cloud patterns, powerful thunderstorms, rainbows, and warm rays of sunshine all declare God's glory. Keep in mind God's glory (the manifestation of God's presence) was not something humans could see and still live. But the sky demonstrates this glory in a way we can observe.

Verse 2. The world of nature continues to sing God's praise through verses 2 and 3. As verse 1 speaks about the sky, so now verse 2 divides the sky into day and night. Not only that, but the days and nights are in conversation with one another. How poetic! It is like what we read in Psalm 8: "When I look up at your skies, at what your fingers made—the moon and the stars that you set firmly in place" (8:3).

Perhaps they are telling one another what happened on the earth in the course of their durations. Or maybe they are singing God's praises. In the next verse, we expect the psalmist to tell us what day said to day and what night said to night.

Verse 3. But we will not find out what day and night are saying up in the sky. The days and nights have been communicating with each other in their own unique ways. "No speech, no words," we read. Their conversations are shrouded in holy mystery. Apparently, it's not for us to hear, or perhaps we "hear" the praises of the sky not with words, but with our eyes.

Verse 4. We know what the sky—day and night—are saying because "their sound extends throughout the world; their words reach the ends of the earth." What a paradox! They speak without words!

But we give the words when we look up at the night sky and say, "Wow! Look how many stars." We sing of God's power when we stand on the porch as the wind picks up and say, "It's going to be a big storm!"

The sun has a starring role (pun intended) in a drama of the sky that starts at the end of verse 4 and continues through verse 6. We will see that the sun serves to praise God. (Recall what we learned about this psalm possibly being an argument against sun worship.)

First, we are told God has given the sun a heavenly tent in the sky. This could refer to the place of the sun's nighttime rest, a place where it goes at night and comes from in the morning.

Verse 5. Next, we learn "the sun is like a groom coming out of his honeymoon suite." This refers to the sun's morning emergence from its nighttime tent. We might chuckle at such a scene today: a bridegroom coming out of the honeymoon suite and into public. But such a display was the cultural norm in ancient Israel. In fact, the whole village would gather in the morning to celebrate the bridegroom's reemergence!

All day long, the sun is like a military warrior thrilled to run its course through the sky with vigor. The connotation is that the sun runs headlong toward the enemy, oblivious to the risk of personal injury.

Verse 6. The sun runs across the sky all day and in the evening returns to the tent God made for it (verse 4). All day long, it has warmed the face of the earth and all that grows. "Nothing escapes its heat." Even in the ancient world, the literary class recognized the people's dependence on the sun, specifically for the growth of plants.

The romantic and heroic language about the sun furthers the drama of the dome above. It is not meant to praise the sun, but rather to characterize the sun's role in giving God glory. Many of the Babylonian and Egyptian hymns of the time honored various sun gods such as Shamash and Aten. In Psalm 19, nature may be personified, but it is not deified.

Verse 7. The focus on nature gives way to a focus on "the LORD's Instruction." We read that the instruction is perfect and that it revives one's being. The implication is that the Law is life-giving, a fundamental force that provides humankind with an inner fuel.

This may be a relatively foreign concept for those who live in cultures where freedom of the will is considered virtuous. Those who resist "too much law" will have a hard time understanding how the Law can be life-giving. But the psalmist pressed the point by telling how the Law is life-giving in six related ways from verses 7-9. It is perfect, faithful, right, pure, correct, and true. Each one of these is paired with its positive effect on human beings.

In addition to "reviving one's very being," the Law is faithful, "making naive people wise." Another way to put it is the Law makes wise the simple. Those who are prone to folly will do well to remember God's Instruction.

Verse 8. Here, we have two more ways the Law benefits humankind. "The LORD's regulations are right," meaning they do not require correction. We can utterly depend on them in every circumstance. This "gladdens the heart" because life can be so complicated. Sometimes the laws of people are not well-written or enforced. But God's law is so right it makes a person glad.

"The LORD's commands are pure, giving light to the eyes." Here we have the light (of the sun?) that shines on our lives through the Lord's commands. As the old adage goes, sunlight is the best disinfectant. God's law exposes what is right and wrong in our lives and thus what is clean or dirty about our hearts.

Verse 9. The last of the pairings comes in verse 9, where we read, "Honoring the LORD" or "the fear of the LORD" has two benefits: It is correct, and it lasts forever. Living by Torah brings a cleanness of heart that endures. Since God's law doesn't change, the blessings of following it won't dissipate in any way.

The final statements of verse 9 summarize and emphasize what we read from verse 7 onward: "The LORD's judgments are true. All of these are righteous." The Law is not righteous because of how expertly it is written. It is righteous because it has its origin in God.

Verse 10. As with the great poetry of the psalms, this poet enlists more rich imagery: gold and honey. Both were treasured commodities in the ancient world, sought and prized by humans. In the same way, the psalmist said people should strive ardently for God's Instructions.

I believe it was Martin Luther who once observed two dogs fighting over a piece of meat. He was heard to say he wished people had the same visceral hunger for God's Word.

You won't find much gold among my possessions, but I do love honey! Every year at the state fair, my family and I love to visit the beehives, where we can safely observe the bees' behavior from the other side of plexiglass and buy little straws of just enough delicious locally- sourced honey to enjoy. You and your class can probably all relate to the richness of good honey, but even wealth or the richest food can't compare with God's law, said the psalmist.

Verse 11. The "great reward" of keeping Torah is not in how it gives us a consequence for every possible bad action, as if it is valuable only as a great set of law books. The great reward comes in keeping Torah, in how it makes people feel knowing they are in harmony with God's purposes for them. Therefore, "there is great reward in keeping them."

In a similar way, Psalm 1:3 says people who "love the LORD's Instruction" are like "a tree planted by streams of water." The blessing of following the Law is not in how it makes us right all the time over other people. It is in how following the Law brings us closer in our relationship with God.

Verse 12. The psalmist even admitted there will be "errors" and "hidden faults" in our following of the Law (NRSV). The Law is perfect, but we are not. We can't always know when we've accidentally broken God's law.

So the last part of verse 12 and the beginning of verse 13 are a plea for forgiveness. It is a return to the understanding that following Torah is about our relationship with God. Though we falter, we can always come to God and seek forgiveness, even if we do not know what we've done wrong.

Verse 13. At the end of verse 12 and going through verse 13, we observe a change in tone. Confidence has given way to advance apology. This does not represent a lessening of the psalmist's faith, however. It was a natural progression as the psalmist realized that following God's Instruction to the letter is humanly impossible. In comparison to the splendor of creation (verses 1-6), the psalmist felt quite insignificant and unworthy.

We can relate to this feeling. We pray God will not judge us by our accidental wrongdoings, for example. We pray that our words, thoughts, and deeds will be acceptable to God (verse 14). We hope with God's help they might be in harmony with the speech of the sky that sings God's praises (verses 2-3).

Verse 14. The final verse of the psalm is a prayer directed at God in the first-person voice. It is probably familiar to you and your class as many preachers quote it as a prayer of illumination before preaching God's Word. The verse is appropriate in such a context because a prayer of illumination asks God to elevate the reading, proclamation, hearing, and response to the Scriptures.

However, the preacher should not mean at heart that God should sanitize whatever the preacher says. God has already given the Law. The preacher is not free to go against God's Instruction under some cover provided by praying the prayer of verse 14.

Just as the psalmist began by extolling the heavenly language of the sky—day to day and night to night—and how it pleases God, so now the psalmist's own words and language must be pleasing to God, too. And we can relate! Who among us does not wish to please God?

Finally, God is described as the psalmist's rock and redeemer. The claim is astounding: God is the divine rock who has built the great earth and heaven above and the great redeemer who forgives even the "unknown sin" (verse 12).

The redeemer figure in the Jewish Holiness Code is actually the one who is the next of kin (Ruth 4:1, 3). So to call God our redeemer is to affectionately declare God is our next of kin, the one who makes it possible for us to live life anew.

Reflect

Say: *Let's begin at the end this time. Let's start our preparation and this Sunday's class with the end of this psalm. Please pray with me:*

> "Let the words of my mouth
>   and the meditations of my heart
>   be pleasing to you,
> Lord, my rock and my redeemer"
> (Psalm 19:14).

This prayer has been prayed from many pulpits over many centuries. It is a favorite because it is scriptural and because we preachers want to stay in our lane, that is, God's Word. We know we can't possibly say everything in a sermon exactly as God wants it said, but we pray we will, with God's help, come as close as possible.

That's what the psalmist wanted to do. He praised God for clearing him of any "unknown sin" or "willful sin" (verses 12, 13). That should cover just about everything so he would "be innocent of any great wrongdoing" (verse 13). In that same spirit let us, as teachers, pray that all we say and think will be pleasing to God.

It isn't often we have a lesson on a psalm. As Gary Thompson reminds us in the student book lesson, psalms are the hymnbook and poetry book of the ancient and modern Israelites.

The psalms continue to be the poetry of the church today. After praying Psalm 19:14 with class members, lead them to discuss the places the psalms show up in their worship and spiritual lives. Ask: *Do we read a psalm in church each Sunday? Is it responsive? Is there a musical refrain?*

Do you have a favorite psalm? Do you have a psalm (in whole or in part) hanging somewhere in your home? Is there one hanging somewhere in the church?

These discussion questions can get the class in the mindset of talking about this psalm on this first Sunday of a new year. Next, you can direct them to Psalm 19 for study.

If you have the *Adult Bible Studies* DVD, play the segment for this lesson. Then ask volunteers to read Psalm 19:1-6.

Say: *The lesson in the student book reminds us of the importance of the psalms to the Jewish people. Psalm 19 appears to have two sections: verses 1-6 about Creation and verses 7-14 about God's Instructions.* Ask:

Did one part speak to you in a special way this week? one verse? Why?

The psalms are so rich in language and imagery that class members will probably point to several places that spoke to them. It is the nature of poetry not always to be linear in its movement. So it's certainly fine for this discussion not to be linear. Sometimes we learn through group exploration.

Here are other questions to prompt the class to explore the psalm together: ***The psalmist talks in verses 1-6 about how the sky proclaims the glory of God. What do you appreciate most when you look at the sky?***

What are the ecological implications of this text? What does the Bible have to say to us here about clean air?

As the sun moves across the sky and "nothing escapes its heat" (verse 6), it serves as a metaphor for God's all-seeing presence. Throughout the Hebrew Bible, the sky has had a role in divine judgment: the Flood, the sulfur that fell on Sodom and Gomorrah, and the shutting off of the heavens during times of famine.

On the other other hand, God uses the sky to provide for the people every day. As our psalm says: "The sky is proclaiming his handiwork" (Psalm 19:1). The rain and sun make the crops grow. It is in the sky that God sets the rainbow, the sign of the covenant between God and the people (Genesis 9:12-17).

Remind the class we have been reading Psalm 19:1-6, so we might "affirm God as the Creator and Sustainer of everything" (the lesson's Purpose Statement). But we have an opportunity to take in the rest of Psalm 19, too.

Explain: ***The rest of Psalm 19 is a wisdom psalm that focuses on God's Instruction, also known as God's law or Torah. Psalm 19:7-14 tells us God's law has great benefits for us. It is like gold or honey.***

Read, or invite someone to read, verses 7-14. I find the best way to read a psalm is slowly, savoring each line of the poetry.

Encourage class members to resist the tendency to confuse the Law with legalism. Too often, Christians throw the whole Old Testament under a charge of legalism, preferring instead the New Testament. But the psalmist reminds us God's law is life-giving. It does not bring us down. It lifts us up, and Jesus did not come to abolish the Law. He came to fulfill it (Matthew 5:17). If anything, Jesus' expectations of us are more intense than the Law (turn the other cheek, love your enemies, let the dead bury the dead, for example).

As we read in Psalm 19, the Law is not an onerous burden, but is instead a source of wisdom, joy, and light (verses 7, 8). God gave us the Law not to be strict, but to make our lives better. It warns us when we are on the wrong path and rewards us when we are on the right path (verse 11).

Psalm 19:10 says of God's Instructions: "They are more desirable than gold—than tons of pure gold! They are sweeter than honey—even dripping off the honeycomb!" Ask: *In what ways have you found God's teachings to be rich and sweet? What does the Law mean for Christians? Is it an antiquated way of life that has been superseded by grace, or is it just as relevant today?*

Acknowledge some Christians have assumed the Old Testament Law is some sort of defective system that had to be replaced by Jesus. But Jesus accepted the Torah and the whole Old Testament as God's authoritative word for himself and for everyone. Who are we, then, to discard it? Besides, it was that kind of supersessionist attitude that has been at the heart of atrocious persecution of Jews over the centuries.

As Christians, we have found the Law was not the fullness of God's revelation to humanity. But that does not make it defective. Christians are expected to live lives of holiness and faith, too. Jesus told his followers, "Unless your righteousness is greater than the righteousness of the legal experts and the Pharisees, you will never enter the kingdom of heaven" (Matthew 5:20). That's an especially high bar!

But Jesus then offered himself as the path to that righteousness, not to replace the Law, but to fulfill it. So Paul could write, "Trusting with the heart leads to righteousness, and confessing with the mouth leads to salvation" (Romans 10:10). Just as following the Law drives us sinners to rely on God's gracious mercy (Psalm 19:12-13), so in following Jesus do we find grace and mercy, for his yoke is easy and his burden is light (Matthew 11:30).

Ask: *What would it look like for you to follow God's law as a Christian? What part of God's law do you find most difficult to follow?*

Close by reminding class members we are not left alone to our own devices in this world. God has ordered the heavens and the sky above (Psalm 19:1-6), and God has given us perfect Instructions. When we fall short—as the psalmist knew we all do (verse 12-13)—we can pray again and again (all together):

Let the words of my mouth
 and the meditations of my heart
 be pleasing to you,
  LORD, my rock and my redeemer (Psalm 19:14).
 Amen.

[1]From *Reflections on the Psalms*, by C. S. Lewis (Harcourt, Brace, and Company, 1986).

The Spiritual Practice of Singing

Praise is one of those church words we hear and use a lot, so much so we may have forgotten what it means. *Praise* is defined as "the act of expressing approval or admiration; commendation; laudation; the offering of grateful homage in words or song, as an act of worship: a hymn of praise to God."[1]

We might feel as though we lack the words to adequately express praise to Almighty God. We want to "get it right." We want God to know of our deep gratitude and love. How can we possibly express to the Creating, Sustaining, Redeeming God what we feel?

Fortunately for us, we have centuries of mothers and fathers in the faith who have lived before us and who have put into words their humble but heartfelt praise to God. When we lack the words to express how we feel and what we want to say, we need look no further than Scripture for help. And to further help us praise God, many now-familiar hymns and choruses come from Scripture. Whether we choose to sing aloud or only in our heads, these words express God alone is worthy of praise.

Just as we cultivate prayer in our lives, we also can cultivate the practice of praise. So grab your Bible and perhaps a hymnal, and dedicate time each day to praising God. As you gather with your class each week, select from the hymns below to sing together or to read aloud the words:

"Holy, Holy, Holy" (*The United Methodist Hymnal*, 64)
"How Great Thou Art" (77)
"Holy God, We Praise Thy Name" (79)
"Let All the World in Every Corner Sing" (93)
"Praise God From Whom All Blessings Flow" (94, 95)
"Praise the Lord Who Reigns Above" (96)
"Praise to the Lord, the Almighty" (139)
"Great Is Thy Faithfulness" (140)
"Majesty, Worship His Majesty" (176)
"All Glory, Laud, and Honor" (280)
"Crown Him With Many Crowns" (327)
"All Praise to Our Redeeming Lord" (554)
"This Is the Day the Lord Hath Made" (658)
"Stand Up and Bless the Lord" (662)
"All Praise to Thee, My God" (682)
"Rejoice the Lord is King," (715, 716)

You may want to find recordings of other hymns and songs of praise and play them for your class. Consider searching YouTube for various renditions of praise songs such as "I Will Sing of the Mercies of the Lord Forever," "Bless the Lord, O My Soul," "Worthy Is the Lamb," "How Great Is Our God," and "Lord, I Lift Your Name on High."

Like prayer, praise can become as natural to us as breathing. Nurture that practice in your life, and help your class to do so as well.

Give thanks to the LORD, call on his name;
   make his deeds known to all people!
Sing to God, sing praises to him;
   dwell on all his wondrous works! . . .
Sing to the LORD, all the earth!
   Share the news of his saving work every single day!
Declare God's glory among the nations;
   declare his wondrous works among all people
   because the LORD is great and so worthy of praise.
He is awesome beyond all other gods
   because all the gods of the nations are just idols,
   but it is the LORD who created heaven!
(1 Chronicles 16:8-9, 23-26)

[1] From *dictionary.com*.

January 9 | Lesson 6
Coming Into God's Presence

Focal Passage
Isaiah 6:1-13

Background Text
Same

Purpose
To respond affirmatively to God's call on our lives

Isaiah 6:1-13

¹In the year of King Uzziah's death, I saw the Lord sitting on a high and exalted throne, the edges of his robe filling the temple. ²Winged creatures were stationed around him. Each had six wings: with two they veiled their faces, with two their feet, and with two they flew about. ³They shouted to each other, saying:

"Holy, holy, holy is the LORD of heavenly forces!
All the earth is filled with God's glory!"

⁴The doorframe shook at the sound of their shouting, and the house was filled with smoke.

⁵I said, "Mourn for me; I'm ruined! I'm a man with unclean lips, and I live among a people with unclean lips. Yet I've seen the king, the LORD of heavenly forces!"

⁶Then one of the winged creatures flew to me, holding a glowing coal that he had taken from the altar with tongs. ⁷He touched my mouth and said, "See, this has touched your lips. Your guilt has departed, and your sin is removed."

⁸Then I heard the Lord's voice saying, "Whom should I send, and who will go for us?"
I said, "I'm here; send me."

⁹God said, "Go and say to this people:
Listen intently, but don't understand;
    look carefully, but don't comprehend.

¹⁰Make the minds of this people dull.

    Make their ears deaf and their eyes blind,

  so they can't see with their eyes

  or hear with their ears,

  or understand with their minds,

  and turn, and be healed."

¹¹I said, "How long, Lord?"
And God said, "Until cities lie ruined with no one living in them, until there are houses without people and the land is left devastated." ¹²The Lord will send the people far away, and the land will be completely abandoned. ¹³Even if one-tenth remain there, they will be burned again, like a terebinth or an oak, which when it is cut down leaves a stump. Its stump is a holy seed.

Key Verse: "Then I heard the Lord's voice saying, 'Whom should I send, and who will go for us?' I said, 'I'm here; send me'" (Isaiah 6:8).

Connect

In Christianity, it's sometimes been affectionately called "the Fifth Gospel." It has inspired great works of art from Handel's "Messiah" to Lee Lawrie's *Wisdom* sculpture over the main entrance to 30 Rockefeller Center to the Isaiah Wall in Bunche Park with the unofficial motto of the United Nations: "They shall beat their swords into plowshares, and their spears into pruninghooks: nation shall not lift up sword against nation, neither shall they learn war any more" (Isaiah 2:4, KJV).

Isaiah is probably the most quoted book of the Old Testament, especially during Advent and Christmas. The suffering servant motif in Isaiah 42; 49; 50; 52 is often applied to Jesus in Christian interpretation. The influence of Isaiah can be seen in Paul's letters in which Isaiah makes up 27 of the 37 quotations of prophets, and the Book of Revelation depends heavily on Isaiah for much of its imagery.

So who was Isaiah, and why was he so influential? The Book of Isaiah tells us at the outset Isaiah, son of Amoz, prophesied during the reigns of four kings of Judah: Uzziah, Jotham, Ahaz, and Hezekiah. This would date his ministry to the middle of the eighth century BC for some 64 years.

From Isaiah's ministry and his call story, we can see he was brave and courageous, unafraid to speak truth to power. But he was not necessarily born with these qualities. We will read in Isaiah 6 how he felt unworthy to be God's prophet. It took a ritual of purification and a direct mandate from God to turn Isaiah into a prophet.

The prophet spoke to God for the people, too. When he learned the harsh message he was to take to the people, he inquired how long God would keep the divine judgment on them. Ultimately, Isaiah knew he answered to God and God alone. As Gary Thompson puts it in the student book, "Old Testament prophets were not primarily prognosticators of future events. Their primary task was to speak to the people on behalf of God."

How desperately people today still need a prophet to call them back to God; and congregations need to let their pastors speak prophetically, which means sometimes hearing a message from the preacher they do not wish to hear. Prophets and prophetic preachers have a greater call on their lives. They answer to a higher power. Remember, Isaiah is highly revered now, but he and his message were not always welcomed by the king or the people during his lifetime.

The emphasis for this lesson and this entire unit is on our capacity to be in awe of God's glory and magnificence. We will read in this passage about how God's glory filled the Temple like smoke. Isaiah could only see as far as the hem of God's robe, not God's own personhood. The Lord was accompanied by supernatural winged angels, one of whom purified Isaiah's mouth with a hot coal from the altar.

The prophet's vision is rich in imagery and sensory input: wings flapping, smoke billowing, door frames rattling. We find ourselves standing behind Isaiah watching him try to take it all in but knowing he can't see God directly and live. But there he is, saying, "I'm here; send me" (Isaiah 6:8).

Isaiah's willingness to accept God's call is an example to us all. We may or may not have a rapturous vision of the throne room of heaven, but we know God's presence in our own lives, and we know what it is to be in awe of God's glory.

Inspect

Our biblical journey takes us to Isaiah, the first of the Major Prophets in the Old Testament. Isaiah sometimes refers to himself as "the prophet" in the book that bears his name, but it's not for certain he wrote the entire Book of Isaiah.

A strong majority of biblical scholars agree the first half of the book (Chapters 1–39) was written by him, but the remainder of the book was written almost two centuries later, immediately before and after the exile in Babylon in the sixth century BC. As Gary Thompson explains in the student book, some scholars have divided these remaining chapters into "Second Isaiah" (Chapters 40–55) and "Third Isaiah" (Chapters 56–66).

The call story of Isaiah we read for this lesson appears to have been written by the prophet himself in the eighth century BC. It comes six chapters into the book. That is unusual for a prophet's call story. (Compare his story to that of Jeremiah and Ezekiel.)

So what comes before and after Isaiah's call story? Chapters 1–12 are largely oracles against Judah. They say God has a plan that will be realized on the Day of Yahweh when Jerusalem will be the central location of God's worldwide reign, but this will happen only after the arrogant king of Assyria is dethroned.

In Isaiah's time, Assyria was expanding westward from what is modern-day Iraq. Assyrian forces destroyed the kingdom of Israel in 722 and 721 BC. Then they subjugated Judah in 701 BC. It was in this military and political morass Isaiah heard the call of God.

Call stories in the Old Testament usually include an encounter with God, a commission to speak God's words or do God's will, and a ritual sign that symbolizes the call. We see this in the call stories of Moses (Exodus 3:1–4:17), Gideon (Judges 6:11-24), Jeremiah (Jeremiah 1:4-10), and Ezekiel (Ezekiel 1:1-3). Of all of these, Isaiah's call story most closely parallels Ezekiel's. Neither of them saw God directly but said they were on the outskirts of a heavenly throne room in which God holds court.

Isaiah 6:1. The story of Isaiah's call begins with a date report: "the year of King Uzziah's death." The exact years of the deaths of Judah's kings are hard to pinpoint, but we figure the death of Uzziah could have been as early as 742 BC or as late as 736 BC. Some scholars have done date calculations (too lengthy to print here) that cast doubt on the historical accuracy of this date report. They suggest the reference to King Uzziah's death is more of a narrative device than it is historical. Uzziah's death marked the rise of King Ahaz and a negative turning point in Judah's diplomacy with Assyria.

Isaiah's awe at the glory of God in the Temple began right away! He saw the Lord sitting "on a high and exalted throne," with the "edges of his robe filling the temple." God is so great Isaiah didn't see or describe God directly. He couldn't even take in all of God's robe, just the edges or the hem.

There would have been no room for Isaiah to stand in the throne room, so he seems to have been watching from the precincts. Some interpreters wonder if the smoke of verse 4 is associated with the great train of the Lord's robe.

Verse 2. "Winged creatures" were in attendance above or around the Lord. These were "seraphs" (NRSV) or seraphim. We find a similar word Numbers 21:6-8 used to describe the poisonous snakes God sent to bite the Israelites. There, the word for "poisonous" could also mean "fiery." So the seraphim have sometimes been likened to fiery flying serpents.

Isaiah tells us the seraphim he saw had six wings. You may recall from our lesson two weeks ago the four living creatures who each had six wings, too (Revelation 4:8). In Isaiah's vision, the angels flew with two wings, covered their eyes with two more wings, and covered their feet (a euphemism for their nakedness) with the remaining two wings. They covered their eyes because no one could see God, and they covered their nakedness because no one should appear naked before the Lord.

Verse 3. Like other heavenly attendants in the Bible, the seraphim praised God with their voices. In this case, they shouted. Their words were a threefold sanctus, a praise based on the word *holy*. This whole verse is repeated several times in daily Jewish services. Your class members will probably remember the "holy, holy, holy" from the recent lesson from Revelation 4 and from the Christian prayer for Holy Communion. Although the hem of God's garment filled the Temple, "all the earth is filled with God's glory."

Verse 4. Many sights and sounds accompanied God's glory. Isaiah reported "the doorframe shook at the sound of their shouting, and the house was filled with smoke." Those who read this account in ancient Israel and Judah would have worried for Isaiah's survival in such a display.

There is symbolic overlap, too, between this heavenly court and the earthly Temple. The shaking of the doorframe could have reminded the first readers of the violent Assyrian military attacks. The smoke could have recalled the smoke of incense and offerings that accompanied Temple worship.

Verse 5. Isaiah's reaction to these powerful displays was not just awe. It was terror and a cry of woe. He literally feared for his life. "I'm ruined" is also translated "I am lost" (NRSV). It could also mean "I am silent," which would serve his point about his unclean lips.

Isaiah dared not join in the heavenly praise because he was "a man with unclean lips," and he was "among a people with unclean lips." He saw himself as no better or no more qualified to be a prophet than anyone else, but he may already have been suspecting he would be called upon to be God's spokesperson.

In some divine call stories, the subject pleads for mercy or makes great vows if God will deliver him. But there's no indication Isaiah was speaking to the Lord or the angels in this verse. Keep in mind it was a Hebrew belief one could not see God and live (Exodus 33:20). So Isaiah's survival amazed him in that way as he said, "Yet I've seen the king, the Lord of heavenly forces" (Isaiah 6:5).

Verse 6. Now an interaction began between Isaiah and the scene he had been witnessing. One of the seraphs flew to him with a lump of coal from the altar, carried with a pair of tongs. It was glowing because of its intense heat.

Fire and heat are powerful biblical symbols often denoting great blessing but also considered uncontrollable. Fire can destroy but also cleanse. It is fascinating and terrifying. Readers of Isaiah will have already encountered the purifying fire in Isaiah 1:25-26.

Verse 7. The seraph touched the hot coal to Isaiah's lips, thus purifying them for speech as God's instrument. We may recoil at the thought of Isaiah's mouth being potentially burned, but there was no such reaction from Isaiah. No healing appears to have been necessary.

Rather, Isaiah received a word of forgiveness and purification. His guilt departed, and his sin was removed. That might sound redundant to us. But guilt and sin had different religious meanings in ancient Temple worship. Guilt was considered not so much a feeling as a state of being that comes from sin. So for guilt and sin to depart was significant. It meant his whole being was undergoing preparation for prophetic ministry.

Verse 8. God spoke for the first time in this narrative. The way God spoke adds to the awe and wonder of the moment. For example, God spoke indirectly (to no one in particular) and did not acknowledge Isaiah's presence. Furthermore, the "us" in "who will go for us" is a divine plural, a literary device a bit like the royal "we" used by a person of high office, such as a king or a pope.

Isaiah must have felt as if he was overhearing deliberations in the divine council. Up to this point, he would not have dared speak up. But the angel had purified him, so he responded, "I'm here; send me." He accepted the divine commission to take God's message to the people, even though he had not yet been told what that message would be or where God's mission would send him.

Verses 9-10. God heard Isaiah's statement of availability and desire to be sent. The "go" of "who will go for us" (verse 8) became "go and say" (verse 9). Isaiah would go "to this people," meaning the people of the covenant. God's language concerning "this people" was distant. It was not the "my people" of happier times.

Read carefully what God said Isaiah should say to this people in verse 9. Did God want them to understand and comprehend the divine words? Actually, no! They should not understand or comprehend. Furthermore, the prophet should go forth to "make the minds of the people dull. Make their ears deaf and their eyes blind, so they can't see with their eyes or hear with their ears, or understand with their minds, and turn, and be healed" (verse 10). Isn't that counterintuitive?

This hardening and dulling would cause the people not to repent. It was not unlike the hardening of Pharaoh's heart in Exodus 9:12. The reason was God had already made the decision to destroy what they had built. The Lord had already found the people refused to listen to the Lord's words or to act with faithfulness. Isaiah's preaching would reinforce their hardness of heart.

Why would God wish to do this? God must have had in mind for the people something more important than healing. Some commentators speculate God may have wanted to preserve divine truth for a future generation since this one had fallen so far from favor. Other commentators suggest God wanted to use the Assyrian conquests to teach the people to return to God, and some point to God's sovereign right to demand obedience. If Isaiah's generation would not listen to God, then God was under no obligation to preserve them.

Verse 11. This verse starts with Isaiah's response to his commission in verses 9-10. "How long, Lord?" Isaiah saw clearly the message he was to bring to the people was a curse. Perhaps the prophet felt concern for the people and hoped the curse did not last long. How long would God hide his face from the house of Jacob (8:17)? Would the curse go on forever, or would the people of God have another chance?

God's answer brought no comfort. The curse of dull minds, deaf ears, and blind eyes would last "until cities lie ruined with no one living in them, until there are houses without people and the land is left devastated." In other words, there would be no reprieve for Judah. God's judgment would result in complete destruction of everything they had built. There would be nothing left to show that civilization ever existed in the Holy City. Since they had fallen out of favor with God, they were to be no longer welcome there. The land would vomit out its inhabitants (Leviticus 18:25).

Verse 12. Unlike some other pronouncements of divine judgment, God did not directly kill members of the population. Rather, the people would be displaced, but they would be completely displaced. There was no allowance for a faithful remnant to remain; "the land will be completely abandoned."

The people of Jerusalem and Judah would be exiled. They would be sent "far away." Interestingly, the Lord did not say here Assyria or Assyria's god would drive the people away. The Lord took full ownership of the decision to exile them.

Verse 13. Not even a tenth of the people would remain in the land. If they did, "they [would] be burned again." One might draw a parallel between the fire-based purification of the prophet's lips and the burning up of the land. It was literally and figuratively a scorched earth policy.

A parable is made out of the trees, especially hardwoods "like a terebinth or an oak." When a tree is burned, it leaves behind a stump. These stumps become "a holy seed." Though God did not speak here of a faithful remnant people who would stay behind, some scholars wonder if those who passed down Isaiah's story may have planted a holy seed of hope in these words.

Reflect

If you have the *Adult Bible Studies* DVD, show the segment related to this lesson.

Believe it or not, plenty of people have had a religious vision. They just don't always talk about it. It may have been in a dream, at night or in the day, or part of an out-of-body or near-death experience.

I read a good book recently by a famed neurologist, the late Oliver Sacks, called *Hallucinations*. He points out how common it is for people to see things they couldn't otherwise verify were there. People with migraines, for example, may see shimmering arcs of light. A simple fever can make one think they are in an earlier time in their lives. In going to sleep or waking from sleep, many of us have had a moment where a dream seemed all too real. People who have lost a loved one sometimes swear they saw him or her in a crowd.

Sacks does not claim religious visions are mere figments of the imagination. He does not doubt the sincerity of anyone who says they have seen an angel, Jesus, or even God. Sacks does not seek to disprove religious visions at all. Rather, he leaves open the distinct possibility they are supernatural encounters with the divine.

If you introduce your class to the topic of hallucinations by explaining how common they are and mention many people have hallucinations they never talk about, someone may volunteer a story of his or her own. Perhaps you as the teacher have a story to share along those lines.

Such an introduction can lead into a discussion about Isaiah's vision in Chapter 6. Ask volunteers to read aloud Isaiah 6:1-13. Ask: ***What do you think of Isaiah's vision in Chapter 6? What imagery jumped out at you?***

Note the focus for this lesson is the awe that comes over us when we consider God's greatness. We don't always need a vision to be in awe of God, but the multisensory nature of Isaiah's vision draws us in. Solicit examples from the class: Look through the vision, particularly the first eight verses, and point out how the five senses are engaged in different parts of the story: sight, hearing, smelling, touching, and tasting.

God's glory filled the Temple like smoke. Isaiah could only see the hem of God's enormous robes. He stood in the outer Temple area, perhaps under a shaking doorframe. Maybe Isaiah had fallen down prostrate on the floor. Ask: ***How do you imagine you would react to such a vision? What words would you use to describe it to others later?***

The point of the story is to establish Isaiah as a prophet. It is a call story. God sought someone to be God's own prophet, but Isaiah knew he was unclean and came from "among a people with unclean lips" (verse 5). Ask: ***Can you relate? Do you feel worthy or unworthy to be*** *another chance?* You may want to explain the political situation using "Inspect."

Explain that God always knows what is best for us. Sometimes that means letting trouble befall us. The people of Judah had to learn a hard lesson. It was the prophet's job to see God's message was told faithfully, whether they wanted to hear that message or not.

Ask: *Has God ever had a message for you that you did not want to hear? What about now? Is there something God has been trying to tell you but you couldn't accept?*

Following a divine call is demanding. I have followed a call to ordained ministry because that is how I (and those who have listened with me) have heard God call me. This is no greater a call than God's intentions for a layperson. All Christians, by virtue of their baptism and the movement of the Holy Spirit, are called into ministry, be it ordained ministry or lay ministry.

Some of my best friends are pastors and others who have answered a call to ordained ministry, too. But I am frequently most moved by laypeople who have responded to God's call. Some have been called to full-time vocational ministry as a layperson. Others devote every waking hour to the service of God, and they aren't paid for it! It comes from their heart, from their response to God's call in their lives.

As you prepare to teach, think about your own call. You have answered God's call to teach. That is no small act of faith! Also consider the members of your class. You may consider saying to them: *I know you might think that you came here today because you just like to come to this class. You came to get something out of this class and the worship service. But you are here because God called you. The Holy Spirit moved you to be here, even if you hadn't considered it that way. You are answering a call just by being here.*

Acknowledge that sometimes people assume they have to have a rapturous vision like Isaiah had. They wait to hear a booming voice tell them what to do. I'm reminded of an episode of a cartoon I once saw in which the main character said something like, "Lord, if you want me to eat this plate of donuts, then don't give me a sign." He waited and nothing happened, so he ate the donuts.

But it doesn't usually work like that. Over the centuries, the church has learned that God's call comes in a variety of forms. Sometimes it is an awe-filled vision. Sometimes there is a voice. Other times the voice of God is mediated through preachers, teachers, and other servants of God's Word. Or the voice might be from a child, a senior saint in the congregation, or from ministry, be it ordained ministry or lay ministry.

God's call is also discerned in the heart. It may be a sound too deep for words, something more akin to a deep-seated feeling. This can be discerned with the counsel of someone who has already had experience discerning God's voice, whether they are themselves clergy or lay.

Call discernment comes when we study call stories in the Bible like Isaiah's. Many a follower of Jesus has heard his words "Follow me" and have answered like Isaiah: "I'm here; send me" (Isaiah 6:8). And some have been surprised to learn God then gave them a message like Isaiah's, an unpopular message people didn't want to hear, a message of God's condemnation. Nevertheless, they cannot escape the call. Like Jeremiah, they feel "a burning fire shut up in [their] bones" (Jeremiah 20:9, NRSV).

Say: *However God calls you today, may you be in awe of God's glory and grace to include you (or any of us) in God's holy work.*

Consider closing by singing or reading together "Here I Am, Lord" by Daniel L. Schutte (*Hymnal*, 593). Then pray together the prayer at the end of the lesson in the student book: **Dear God, much like the days of Isaiah, we live in chaotic times. Forgive us when we fail to hear and respond to your call upon our lives and when we fail to live by your laws. Show us how to live faithfully each day; in Jesus' name we pray. Amen.**

Questions We Ask of the Bible

Reading, interpreting, and teaching the Bible is hard! Let's admit it. Adult Sunday school teachers sometimes tell curriculum writers and editors the material is difficult. Their students often have questions they don't know how to answer. So let's see if we can make this a little easier by breaking down the kind of questions we often ask of the Bible.

First, we need to learn a new term: *biblical criticism*. No, that doesn't mean being critical (negative) about the Bible! Instead, it's like literary criticism. In literary criticism, people read books and then digest what they've read. They consider the time period in which the book was written. They think about what the author's intention might have been in writing the book. Who was its original audience? Sometimes we read books, and we feel as if we're missing something, like a sense of the time period or as if a chapter is missing. So the reader draws conclusions about the work.

This is literary criticism. It has nothing to do with whether we liked the book. It is about what kind of questions we are asking of the book. So in biblical criticism, we do the same thing with the Bible. We ask certain questions of the biblical text we read; and like literary criticism, our questions in biblical criticism are not "Did I like it?" Our questions are more around things such as, "Who wrote this part?" "What exactly did the writer mean here?" "How does this compare with other parts of the Bible that I've read?"

For every kind of question we can ask of a Bible text (and there are many!), we have a category of biblical criticism. There's only enough room here to cover the most frequently used categories.

So let's start with textual criticism. These are the kind of questions we ask when we remember the Bible was not written in modern English. It was originally written in Hebrew, Greek, and a little Aramaic. Many scholars for many years have compared different ancient scrolls of Scripture and looked at the differences and similarities. That's textual criticism.

To be honest, most of the textual criticism work has already been done for us by the translators of our English Bible. But sometimes they put little notes at the bottom of the pages that say things such as, "Hebrew uncertain." And once in a while in preaching and teaching, people like me say, "What the Greek here really means is. . . ." That's textual criticism.

Another kind of biblical criticism is historical criticism. These are questions that arise about—you guessed it—history. What were things like in Bible times? How do we understand the text in its historical location?

A whole lot has changed since the books of the Bible were written. There are some idioms, for example, used when the Bible was written that we have to guess at today. Think

Enrichment Material 71

of it this way: Imagine if 3,000 years from now someone uncovered a fragment of a newspaper with a political cartoon on it. Suppose they had no idea an elephant was meant to represent Republicans and a donkey was meant to represent Democrats. Assume information had been lost over time. What would they think when they read the cartoon? Would they have any idea what they were looking at? Would they even suppose animals talked out loud thousands of years ago?

Sometimes we have to piece together things from Bible times that are not at all obvious. That's historical criticism.

Let's look at just one more major kind of biblical criticism today: source criticism. Here, we have to hear a hard truth: The fact of the matter is we have no original manuscripts from any of the Bible writers. What we have are copies of copies of copies (at least!), most of which come from the medieval period!

And remember the stories of the Old and New Testaments come from an oral tradition. Few people knew how to read and write. Furthermore, after Jesus' life and ministry, a lot of his followers believed he would come back in their lifetimes. So why would they bother writing down all the things he said?

They didn't. Not for a long time. And they wrote them down from memory or sometimes from what someone else told them. Since there was no printing press, each Gospel and letter had to be copied down by hand. All of these are factors in source criticism, which asks, "Where did this text come from? Who copied it down? Did they have an agenda?"

If you subscribe to the theory that humans have a tendency to mess things up over time, then you have to figure the oldest manuscripts are the most accurate to what the original Bible writers put down. Don't get me wrong! I believe God inspired not just those who first wrote down the words of the Bible, but also those who preserved them, copied them, recopied them, and who even today decide which ones are most reliable when developing new Bible translations. This is not a commentary on biblical inspiration.

I'm just giving you a few categories for some of those questions you probably get in class from time to time. Even if you don't have the answer to every question (and not even Bible scholars have that), you can at least help the class think through the question they are trying to answer. And you can't get to an answer if you can't agree on what the question is!

All of these are different kinds of biblical criticism (again, that doesn't mean being "critical of the Bible"). But these remind us there are a lot of legitimate questions that will come to our minds when we study Scripture. We will do well if we can at least categorize these questions and keep our classes focused on what we're asking of a particular Bible text.

January 16 | Lesson 7
The Transfiguration

Focal Passage
Mark 9:2-8

Background Text
Mark 9:2-13

Purpose
To understand how listening to God can radically change our lives

Mark 9:2-8

²Six days later Jesus took Peter, James, and John, and brought them to the top of a very high mountain where they were alone. He was transformed in front of them, ³and his clothes were amazingly bright, brighter than if they had been bleached white. ⁴Elijah and Moses appeared and were talking with Jesus. ⁵Peter reacted to all of this by saying to Jesus, "Rabbi, it's good that we're here. Let's make three shrines—one for you, one for Moses, and one for Elijah." ⁶He said this because he didn't know how to respond, for the three of them were terrified.

⁷Then a cloud overshadowed them, and a voice spoke from the cloud, "This is my Son, whom I dearly love. Listen to him!" ⁸Suddenly, looking around, they no longer saw anyone with them except Jesus.

Key Verse: "Then a cloud overshadowed them, and a voice spoke from the cloud, 'This is my son, Whom I dearly love. Listen to him!'" (Mark 9:7).

Connect

In this unit of lessons we are looking at some of the most awe-filled stories of the Bible. But what makes a story awe-filled? Is it an otherworldly vision? Something like divine special effects?

Certainly, the more miraculous, apocryphal, and visually intricate stories of the Bible inspire awe in us. But if that is all they were designed to do, then the stories would just be about tricks or special effects. No, the stories that rock us back on our heels have to point to something beyond themselves. They are about God—Father, Son, and Holy Spirit—who is greater than anything we can capture in a vision, story, or description.

The awe-inspiring stories of the Bible are one of God's ways of getting and keeping our attention. But that's just the start. In the Gospel of John, the miracles are usually called "signs" because they point the way toward the Savior, Jesus Christ. And in each sign there is practical purpose and metaphorical meaning.

Ironically, John is the only Gospel not to include a story of the Transfiguration of Jesus. One would think John would seize on the story because it depicts the glory and divinity of Jesus, something John was keen to focus on in his telling of the Jesus story. But we find the Transfiguration in the Synoptic Gospels (Matthew, Mark, and Luke).

It is a story many students of the Bible probably know already. When we teach a familiar story, part of our challenge is to make it seem fresh again. So this lesson focuses on the (quite literal) awesomeness of the story. We will let the glory of Jesus shine for itself, but we will examine why Jesus would be so arrayed in light and accompanied by Elijah and Moses. What is Mark trying to tell us through his version of the story? What was Jesus trying to convey to Peter, James, and John—and to us today?

We may be tempted to mentally categorize and shelve the Transfiguration story as one of those "strange things that happened in the Bible but doesn't happen anymore." But let us resist that temptation by receiving the story as it is, taking nothing away from its glory. We will need to engage our mind's eye and our spiritual imaginations so we will not just observe Jesus' transfiguration but also witness Jesus in his glory. This story is a faith-building gift from God!

If you are like me, you need to go back to awe-filled stories such as the Transfiguration sometimes. Life can be difficult, and we need to be reminded Jesus is Lord! What better way to do than to see Jesus in glory among the heroes of the Old Testament? Like Peter, we may want to build shrines or tents of meeting and stay there forever, basking in the great light of Jesus' glory.

Hopefully, after we examine the Transfiguration in this lesson, you and your class will carry the story around with you in your everyday life. You may be pleasantly surprised to see it come back into your mind's eye when you need inspiration and reassurance God is in control.

So journey up the mountain with Jesus, Peter, James, and John this week in your preparation, and take your class along for the journey when you meet. Be ready to be amazed, for Peter was right when he said, "It's good that we're here" (Mark 9:5)!

Inspect

We call this story "The Transfiguration of Jesus" because the King James Version says, "He was transfigured before them" (Mark 9:2, KJV). But some translations or paraphrases say "transformed" (CEB) or "his appearance changed" (*The Message*). If it's difficult to translate the Greek word (*metamorphothe*, pronounced meta-MORPH-oh-thay), it is because the whole Transfiguration event is so hard to describe or explain.

It's not that the Synoptic Gospels differ much in how they tell the story. It is found in Matthew 17:1-8; Luke 9:28-36; and in the text for this lesson. Essentially, three disciples (Peter, James, and John) were taken to a mountain where Jesus' external appearance changed before them to become magnificently bright. Moses and Elijah then appeared with Jesus, and Peter suggested three booths or tents be built for them. A voice spoke from a cloud, named Jesus as the Son of God, and said, "Listen to him" (Mark 2:7)! Then Jesus was alone again with the three disciples.

Small differences do exist between the Gospel accounts. Luke tells us Jesus, Moses, and Elijah were talking about "Jesus' departure, which he would achieve in Jerusalem" (Luke 9:31). Luke also says all three disciples "were almost overcome with sleep" (Luke 9:32). Mark tells us Peter was terrified.

In Matthew, Jesus helps them to their feet and tells them not to be afraid. And Luke suggests the disciples and Jesus spent the night on the Mount of Transfiguration (Luke 9:37). Scholars believe the similarities between the accounts make them likely to be historically accurate despite these minor differences.

The Transfiguration is a critical and central event in the story of Jesus of Nazareth. It is a theological testimony to Jesus' identity as the Son of God. The voice of God is heard as it was at Jesus' baptism (Matthew 3:13-17; Mark 1:9-11; Luke 3:21-23). Like Moses whose face radiated light after he caught a glimpse of God's glory (Exodus 34:29-35), Jesus fully radiated God's glory and was flanked by the central figures of the Law (Moses) and the prophets (Elijah). (Watch for Moses' story next week!)

Church tradition has held Mount Tabor as the site of Jesus' transfiguration. Some scholars have suggested mounts Meron, Nebo, or Hermon. But the symbolism of the mountain is as (or more) important than its location. Biblical mountains generally symbolize a meeting place between heaven and earth. Theophanies (visible manifestations of God) usually happen on mountains and are often accompanied by light, wind, smoke, and/or the divine voice. This is how we began to use the term *mountaintop experience* to describe a sublime spiritual encounter with God.

Mark 8:27–9:1. Immediately before Mark's story of Jesus' transfiguration, we read Jesus and the disciples had gone "into the villages near Caesarea Philippi" (Mark 8:27) when a discussion occurred about Jesus' identity. Jesus asked, "Who do people say that I am" (8:27), and they answered, "Some say John the Baptist, others Elijah, and still others one of the prophets" (8:28). Jesus then confronted Peter with the same question. Peter answered, "You are the Christ" (8:29).

This discussion in Mark about the identity of Jesus serves as a lead-in to the Transfiguration account. Peter, James, and John would have the answer to the question of Jesus' true identity when they saw Jesus in his glory and heard the Father's identification of him as "my Son, whom I dearly love" (9:7).

Mark 9:2. Just as six days passed for Moses on the mountain before God spoke (Exodus 24:16), so six days passed before "Jesus took Peter, James, and John." After all, Jesus is depicted as God's new chosen leader for Israel.

This marks the second of four times when Peter, James, and John were alone with Jesus for a significant event. The first was in Mark 5:37 for the raising of Jairus's daughter. We find the third in Mark 13:3, when they questioned Jesus about his prediction of the Temple's destruction. The final occasion is recorded in Mark 14:33, when Jesus took them further into the garden of Gethsemane to wait while he prayed. Thus Mark gives us the distinct impression Peter, James, and John were particularly close to Jesus.

In this text, they were alone with Jesus on "the top of a very high mountain" (9:2). Mark used extra Greek adjectives to emphasize how high and set apart they were. He had a tendency to portray Jesus and his disciples as being in private gatherings for some of the more significant events in Jesus' ministry.

Mark wasted no time in telling us Jesus "was transformed in front of them" (9:2). While Matthew and Mark used the word that literally means he assumed a different form, Luke avoided the word and said instead, "The appearance of his face changed and his clothes flashed white like lightning" (Luke 9:29).

In the Old Testament and old Jewish literature, it was said the righteous would someday take on a new heavenly form (Daniel 12:3; 2 Esdras 7:97). In the New Testament, Paul used the same Greek verb to say how we should "be transformed by the renewing of your minds" (Romans 12:2) and how "we are being transformed into that same image from one degree of glory to the next degree of glory" (2 Corinthians 3:18). He also used it when he wrote about the glorious bodies of the believers in 1 Corinthians 15 and Philippians 3:21.

Despite the use of this same word in other places in the Bible, however, the Transfiguration of Jesus is in a category all its own. For we are told that . . .

Verse 3. "his clothes were amazingly bright, brighter than if they had been bleached white." Interestingly, Mark did not use a Greek word specifically for "bleach," but rather referred to a launderer, saying literally, "His garments became shining white, exceedingly, as a launderer on earth cannot whiten." This literal translation shows us how our Bible translators have helped us interpret what Mark meant. Note Mark also did not state Jesus' face ever shined (the way Matthew and Luke described it).

We do see other places in the Bible where the clothing of the saints is said to shine, especially in apocalyptic literature such as Daniel 12:3 and Revelation 4:4; 7:9. Daniel's vision of the "ancient one" also comes to mind where it was said "his clothes were white like snow; his hair was like a lamb's wool" (Daniel 7:9). The Greeks and Romans even had stories of gods such as Demeter shining and filling a house with light or Apollo taking the appearance of Lycaon.

Mark doesn't give us a direct explanation of the meaning of this change in Jesus' appearance. Was this the divine glory of Jesus breaking through the veil of his humanity? Is it a glimpse of a form Jesus will take in his future coming (Mark 8:38)? Mark leaves his audience to ponder such questions.

Verse 4. Jesus was joined by Elijah and Moses. Specifically, we are told they "appeared." Mark used the same word here he and Luke used for the appearances of angels, the resurrected Jesus, and other supernatural encounters.

The appearance of Jesus' two Old Testament companions has traditionally been interpreted to mean he was supported by the Law (Moses) and the Prophets (Elijah). Moses had promised the Lord would raise up "a prophet like me from your community, from your fellow Israelites. He's the one you must listen to" (Deuteronomy 18:15). And it was said Elijah would appear "before the great and terrifying day of the LORD arrives" (Malachi 4:5).

Don't you wish we could have had a transcript of what the three of them were saying? Luke's account gives us our only hint when it says they "spoke about Jesus' departure" (Luke 9:31).

Verse 5. In keeping with Peter's character, he reacted to all of this by blurting out that three shrines be made: "One for you, one for Moses, and one for Elijah." Mark even felt he had to explain Peter's outburst by saying "he didn't know how to respond" (verse 6) because he, James, and John were terrified. James and John did not say anything. But to Peter's credit, he called Jesus Rabbi, and he knew something significant was happening.

The CEB says Peter wanted to make three shrines. The NRSV says "dwellings" (Mark 9:5) with a note the word might also be translated "tents." A literal translation would be "tents," "booths," or "huts." But Peter was alluding to the tent of meeting in the wilderness (or the Tabernacle) in which humans encountered the Lord God. It might be Peter wasn't even clear in his own mind what he meant because . . .

Verse 6. "He said this because he didn't know how to respond." All three of the disciples were frightened, so perhaps all three of them "didn't know how to respond." We will see a similar response from those same three disciples when Jesus was praying in the garden of Gethsemane. The second time he came to them, he found them sleeping, and Mark says, "They didn't know how to respond to him" (Mark 14:40).

Their fear could have been a simple primal reaction of self-preservation, or it could have been more of a religious awe. Keep in mind, though, up to this point in the Gospel, the disciples have not shown a great deal of understanding around Jesus' predictions of suffering and death. And on the way down the mountain, they wondered, "What's this 'rising from the dead'" (9:10). So any real insight into what was going on might have come later when Mark wrote down his Gospel.

Though they were terrified and Peter blurted out a premature idea, there is no indication Peter's reaction upset Jesus like it did just a few verses back when he said, "Get behind me, Satan" (Mark 8:33).

Verse 7. Two things happened next: A cloud overshadowed them, and a voice spoke.

The cloud is a typical biblical sign of divine presence and a theophany, a human encounter with God. Some early church interpreters saw the cloud as the presence of the Holy Spirit, though the text does not indicate this.

We're reminded of similar occurrences in the Old Testament. God told Moses, "I'm about to come to you in a thick cloud in order that the people will hear me talking with you so that they will always trust you" (Exodus 19:9). On Moses' third day on Mount Sinai, there was "a thick cloud on the mountain" (Exodus 19:16). And in Exodus 40:35, a cloud settled on the tent of meeting such that Moses could not enter it.

The heavenly voice echoed the words spoken to Jesus at his baptism: "You are my Son, whom I dearly love; in you I find happiness" (Mark 1:11). But in this case, the voice was speaking to the disciples.

As Gary Thompson wrote in the student book, "God not only spoke to Jesus on the mountain that day of the Transfiguration; God also spoke to Peter, James, and John, who were with him that day. Jesus invited them to go with him to the mountaintop because he was training them, mentoring them, teaching them by his example. One important lesson they needed to learn was to listen for the voice of God." The Transfiguration was for them and is also for those who read about it thousands of years later.

The disciples then and now are given a direct order: "Listen to him" (9:7)! That means hearing as well as obeying. Recall Moses saying the Lord would raise up a prophet and "he's the one you must listen to" (Deuteronomy 18:15). And notice God did not introduce Moses or Elijah at all, symbolizing Jesus' special relationship with God.

Remember in the previous chapter of Mark, Jesus predicted his passion and encountered pushback from Peter and the other disciples (Mark 8:27-38). So Mark's readers can pick up on a rising intensity in the story. Jesus was in more and more peril. Now they needed reassurance Jesus is indeed the Messiah. They found reassurance in the Lord God's words: "This is my Son" (9:7). God's favor still rests on Jesus, and Jesus will ultimately be vindicated for all his sufferings.

Verse 8. Elijah and Moses disappeared in an instant. Presumably, the cloud disappeared, too. The Ttransfiguration event came to an abrupt end.

Our English translations lose some of the redundancy of the original Greek in which Mark wrote, "They no longer saw anyone" and "only Jesus was with them." The writers of Mark's time didn't use punctuation, underline, bold, or italics for emphasis. They used repetition. So this was Mark's way of emphasizing Jesus' singular role in accomplishing the redemptive work of God. Elijah, Moses, and the voice of God were there to bear witness to Jesus as the Son of God.

Verse 9. This verse (beyond the Focal Passage for this lesson) recounts how Jesus, Peter, James, and John came down from the mountain. Furthermore, it captures Jesus' instruction that they were "not to tell anyone what they had seen until after the Human One had risen from the dead."

Just as we took note of the mountain symbolism in verse 2 when they ascended, we see the meaning of their descent down the mountain. They were returning to the regular everyday world. But they had witnessed something that changed them forever. We might imagine the three disciples descending the mountain with a greater spiritual maturity and understanding of Jesus' messiahship.

However, they were to be prevented from telling anyone what they saw. Scholars refer to this kind of instruction as Jesus' "messianic secret." There are four ways in Mark in which Jesus deliberately suppressed the message he is the Messiah:

- When Jesus told the demons to stay silent about him (Mark 1:25, 34).
- When Jesus told people not to talk about it (1:43-45; 5:43; 7:36; 8:30; 9:9).
- When Jesus withdrew from the crowds to give special teaching (4:34; 7:17).
- When Jesus taught in parables to conceal the mystery of the kingdom of God from outsiders (4:10-12).

There are various theories as to why Jesus would tell them to remain silent. Perhaps Jesus was not wanting to attract negative attention from his critics until it was his time to be crucified; or maybe Jesus didn't want his followers to jump to conclusions regarding the Transfiguration until they had come to see his whole ministry, death, and resurrection. Some interpreters wonder if Mark added these "messianic secret" passages to keep Jesus' messiahship from being revealed until after his resurrection.

Reflect

Ahead of time, if you have the *Adult Bible Studies* DVD, preview the segment for this lesson, and determine at what point you will show it to your class.

Few scenes in the Bible are more awe-inspiring than Jesus' transfiguration. It's an event that defies imagination. Add to this the "messianic secret" (described at the end of "Inspect") and how the story of the Transfiguration must have been told only by Peter, James, and/or John after Jesus' resurrection.

So visual artists, for example, have been confounded in their attempts to capture Jesus' divine appearance on the mountain. We even get the impression from the Synoptic Gospel writers (Matthew, Mark, and Luke) they were grasping at ways to try to describe what Jesus looked like. How do you make Jesus' clothes appear "amazingly bright, brighter than if they had been bleached white" (Mark 9:3)?

Since the Transfiguration is a visual event, however, you might consider looking at artistic depictions through Internet image searches. Try reproducing these in class (printed, on a screen, or on phones) to facilitate class discussion. But emphasize the supernatural nature of the Transfiguration and how artists have struggled to depict it.

I recommend *The Transfiguration* by Raphael, which was actually the master's last painting at the young age of 37. Compare this to the Transfiguration icon by Theophanes the Greek. In most icons of Jesus' transfiguration, Elijah and Moses are floating above the disciples in relatively serene poses, while Peter, James, and John are sprawling or writhing below.

If you display an artist's rendering of the Transfiguration to your class, ask: ***What do you notice about how the artist depicts the transfiguration of Jesus? Is it similar to how you imagine it? Why or why not?***

This entry point into a discussion of the Transfiguration will allow you to set the story in the context of this unit on awe. Ask volunteers to read aloud Mark 9:1-8. Review the details of this experience, inserting helpful observations from "Inspect" and things you have noticed. Ask: *In what ways is Jesus' transfiguration awe-inspiring to you?*

Class members may also find an entry point into the story through the characters of Peter, James, and/or John. Peter is clearly the most vocal of the three. Perhaps you or some of your students feel you would be like Peter in this story. *Do you have a tendency to try to make sense of something that doesn't make sense at first?* It's safe to say we all do that.

Suggest to the class we should not be too hard on Peter. He was stupefied. They all were. And who wouldn't want to hold onto a perfect moment like Jesus' transfiguration, complete with the dearly beloved Elijah and Moses? Peter's idea wasn't entirely crazy. He meant honor and respect. But, ultimately, he had to learn he already had a tent of meeting or shrine to God right there in Jesus of Nazareth.

Ask if any in your class think they would react more like James or John. Some people prefer to take in a theophany and ponder it as we saw Zechariah, Elizabeth, and Mary do in the annunciations of Lessons 1 and 2. Ask: *With which disciple do you most identify? Are you a Peter? a James? a John? Why?*

However we get into the Transfiguration event, we come away changed. It may be a familiar story to most of your students now, so challenge them to imagine the Gospels without the Transfiguration. Ask: *If none of the Gospel writers had included the account of Jesus' transfiguration, what would we be missing? How would your conception of Jesus be lesser or different?*

Remind the class the Transfiguration is generally classified as a miracle, but one that happened to Jesus instead of to someone else. Some interpreters have said the Transfiguration was not a new thing that happened to Jesus so much as it was a "pulling back of the veil" on Jesus' true nature. They suggest the transfigured Jesus serves as a preview of the later resurrected Jesus.

The glory of Jesus on the Mount of Transfiguration was awe-inspiring to be sure. Though Mark did not describe Jesus' personal appearance like Matthew 17:2 and Luke 9:29, Mark does say, "His clothes were amazingly bright, brighter than if they had been bleached white" (Mark 9:3).

Adding to the awe of the event was the appearance of Elijah and Moses. We're not sure why, but Mark mentions Elijah first while Matthew and Luke name Moses first. In any event, the appearance of these two giants of the Old Testament took the scene to a new level. It was said that both great men had not died. Rather, according to legend, Moses had been taken up in a cloud. And Elijah "went to heaven in a windstorm" at the conclusion of his earthly ministry (2 Kings 2:11).

Ask: *What do you believe is the significance of the appearance of Elijah and Moses? What do you imagine they were saying to Jesus?*

Suggest another way in which we are in awe of the Transfiguration is in the cloud and the voice that says, "This is my Son, whom I dearly love. Listen to him" (Mark 9:7). This is one of several similarities between Jesus' Transfiguration and the experiences of Moses on Mount Sinai in Exodus 24, 33, and 34 (the text for the next lesson). Others include the six days (Mark

9:2; Exodus 24:16), the transformed appearance (Mark 9:3; Exodus 34:30), and the reaction of fear (Mark 9:6; Exodus 34:30).

It's difficult to discern what the tone of the divine voice was like. Was it comforting in that the message was similar to the one Jesus heard in his baptism: "You are my Son, whom I dearly love; in you I find happiness" (Mark 1:11)? Or was it a reprimand of the disciples who had just rejected Jesus' Passion prediction in Mark 8:27-38? After all, the Transfiguration event happened not long after Jesus said, "Get behind me, Satan" to Peter (8:33). Perhaps the disciples needed to start thinking "God's thoughts" instead of "human thoughts" (8:33), and that's why Jesus was transfigured.

Affirm that for the first disciples, the Transfiguration was a demonstration of Jesus' glory. It was a foretaste of the Resurrection. To fearful disciples it was a reminder they were backing the true Messiah. The Transfiguration proves Jesus is greater than Elijah or Moses who stood by him, not the other way around. Jesus is not a return of Elijah or one of the prophets as some had just said in Mark 8:28. He is the only one left standing on the "stage" after his Transfiguration. He is the Messiah!

Ask: *What do you think the Transfiguration was meant to teach the three disciples who saw it? What do you think it was meant to teach those who read about it later? What is it meant to teach you about Jesus today?*

Point out that just as there was a time when Peter, James, and John ascended the mountain before they had seen Jesus' glory, so too was there a time they descended the mountain back into the valley of their ministry with Jesus. Encourage class members to describe their own mountaintop and valley experiences. Note, following Jesus is not just a matter of going from mountaintop to mountaintop. Psalm 84:7 reminds us those who are in the Lord's dwelling place "go from strength to strength." But some days, we would be glad to just be in one place of strength!

Ask: *How can the Transfiguration account give you encouragement and hope today? How can you stand in awe of Jesus, even now as you read about the event?*

If you worship with a church that follows the Revised Common Lectionary, the story of the Transfiguration according to Luke will be your Gospel reading in a few weeks. Though the details are a little different (as outlined at the start of "Inspect"), the story is basically the same. Every year, in fact, this story is read on the last Sunday before the start of Lent. It is our one last time to glimpse into Jesus' great glory before we follow him to the cross and see his glory again in the Resurrection.

Ask: *How does the Transfiguration story anticipate or foreshadow Jesus' resurrection? Where do you feel awe in both events?*

Close by praying together the prayer at the end of the lesson in the student book: **Dear God, help us open our hearts and minds to sense your presence, to feel your love, and to hear your voice. Help us comprehend the mission you give us and renew our commitment to your call; in Jesus' name we pray. Amen.**

How to Look Past What's Right in Front of Us

The biblical texts for the lessons in Unit 2 feature a lot of visionary language. We find Isaiah being swept up to the heavenly realm to see God's throne room (Lesson 6). We see Peter, James, and John witnessing Jesus' transfiguration in such a way that our Gospel writers can hardly describe it (Lesson 7). Moses comes from his encounter with God with a supernatural glow on his face (Lesson 8). Finally, we find John in some kind of visionary trance as he hears a choir of angels (Lesson 9).

So why do most of us go through life in a relatively mundane way compared to these people? Save for a few people who claim to have had out-of-body experiences or who have "enhanced" their imaginations by some questionable means, the vast majority of us have trouble relating to these supernatural, otherworldly experiences, myself included.

We might feel as if we're missing out. Maybe there's something wrong with us, we wonder. And sure enough, there are some preachers who tell people they have to have some kind of spiritual trance to have received the Spirit of God. Don't misunderstand me! Some people have had mystical experiences given to them by God. And the last thing I would do is doubt them because it's not my place to question what God might do.

But on the whole, for those of us in the vast majority who have not had such experiences, we need to keep in mind our experience of God is no less legitimate. Remember God came to us in Jesus—an incarnate person, which means "in the flesh." Would God have come to us in the flesh if God had insisted all of our divine experiences be mystical and otherworldly? No!

One factor we should keep in mind when reading these visions and strange experiences in the Bible is that the Bible was written before the Age of Enlightenment that started in Europe in the seventeenth and eighteenth centuries. Since the time of the Enlightenment, there has been a whole shift toward emphasizing the reason and the senses as the primary sources of knowledge. In other words, the Enlightenment thinkers said, if you can't see it, feel it, and understand it, "it isn't really real."

But before the Enlightenment, people didn't generally think that way. If you claimed to have had a vision, few people would contradict you. And your vision (no matter what it was about) could be considered as real as the chair I'm sitting in while I write this.

Let's not get into an argument over which way is better. The point is the visions we read about in the Bible were written down a long time before the Age of the Enlightenment. The point is people in Bible times didn't ask the same questions about the visions we'd ask today. Visions were sources of knowledge just as valid as we consider science to be today.

When we read about visions and transfigurations and premonitions and such things in the Bible, we need to take a pause before we start imposing post-Enlightenment questions on them. That's not fair to the people who had and recorded those visions. We have to start by just taking them at face value and practice humility ourselves. Who are we to assume we know how one can and can't experience a vision from God?

January 23 | Lesson 8

Beholding God's Glory

Focal Passage
Exodus 34:29-35

Background Text
Same

Purpose
To strengthen our resolve to make listening to God a priority

Exodus 34:29-35
²⁹Moses came down from Mount Sinai. As he came down from the mountain with the two covenant tablets in his hand, Moses didn't realize that the skin of his face shone brightly because he had been talking with God. ³⁰When Aaron and all the Israelites saw the skin of Moses' face shining brightly, they were afraid to come near him. ³¹But Moses called them closer. So Aaron and all the leaders of the community came back to him, and Moses spoke with them. ³²After that, all the Israelites came near as well, and Moses commanded them everything that the Lord had spoken with him on Mount Sinai. ³³When Moses finished speaking with them, he put a veil over his face. ³⁴Whenever Moses went into the Lord's presence to speak with him, Moses would take the veil off until he came out again. When Moses came out and told the Israelites what he had been commanded, ³⁵the Israelites would see that the skin of Moses' face was shining brightly. So Moses would put the veil on his face again until the next time he went in to speak with the Lord.

Key Verse: "After that, all the Israelites came near as well, and Moses commanded them everything that the Lord had spoken with him on Mount Sinai" (Exodus 34:32).

Connect

Have you ever seen someone who had a "glow" about them? I remember how my wife glowed when she was pregnant with each of our daughters. I'm sure I was biased, but I saw it! Others said they did, too. In fact, my wife has an uncanny ability to see it in other women. Before a friend ever announces that she's pregnant, my wife has already whispered to me, "I think she's expecting!"

Other people have a glow about them when they are carrying around a bit of good news. Perhaps they've been offered a promotion, or they're excited about an upcoming vacation. There's a light inside that just keeps radiating out from their countenance.

Some people just radiate God's peace and presence. Maybe they've just come from a spiritual retreat. Perhaps they are coming out of their "prayer closet" time. Or it could happen after they've been in worship with other Christians. Time spent with the invisible God can just seem to be visible in them.

In this unit of lessons, we're focusing on the awe-inspiring presence of God. We're reading accounts of God's glory. Whether it's Isaiah's vision of God's robes filling the Temple or the moment Jesus was transfigured before Peter, James, and John, God's glory evokes awe and wonder. And wherever the glory of God is, there's a lot of shining!

But the text for this lesson is different. In this instance, God's glory was not limited to the Temple or the Mount of Transfiguration or Mount Sinai. In Exodus 34:29-35, we find out God's glory was reflected on Moses' very face. I can't think of any other account in the Bible in which an individual physically reflected the glory of God like that.

The account of Moses' shining face is fascinating and inspirational. It's the story of God giving the people of Israel a new gift: a renewed covenant after the whole golden calf debacle. As Gary Thompson writes in the student book, "One of the lessons the people of Israel had to learn, and one we must also learn, is that while God is a God of grace, compassion, and love, God also makes arduous demands and requires total allegiance. An important part of their ongoing relationship with God was confession, repentance, and forgiveness."

Rather than creating awe in the people by the thunder and lightning of Mount Sinai, God decided to let the divine glory come among the people by way of Moses' person. This was unprecedented in Hebrew Scripture. For Christians, it serves as a prefiguring of the way God would eventually come among us in the person of Jesus Christ.

God's glory (and the awe that comes with it) belongs to God alone, and God is under no compulsion to show it to us. But out of compassion and grace, God gave the Israelites another chance and let the glory come among them.

We will also explore the notion of Moses' veil. As you've read, when Moses finished telling the people what God said, he veiled his face. He would then take off the veil when he was in the Lord's presence and when he would come out to deliver a word from the Lord. But in between those times, he would put the veil back on.

The matter of the veil reminds us God's glory is, generally speaking, quite hidden from us. As the Hebrews often said, you can't look at the Lord God and live. Moses even had to get into a gap in the rock on the mountain and hide his face while God passed by, leaving only a trail of glory for Moses to see (Exodus 33:19-23). And Moses' face shone just from that ever-so-slight exposure.

We may only ever see a distant reflection of God's glory in this life. But the good news is we don't have to be Moses to reflect God's glory, at least in so far as God shows it to us. Even from just the smallest amount of God's glory that has been revealed to us, we stand in awe. We may not shine the way Moses did, but we are bearers of God's presence in the world by the grace of the Holy Spirit.

Inspect

What do you think of when you think of the Book of Exodus? *The Ten Commandments*, the film with Charlton Heston? The story of the escape from Egypt? We find those events in the first half of Exodus (Chapters 1–19). The second half is about the covenant between the Lord and the people, brought to them by Moses (Chapters 20–40).

After they escaped Pharaoh, the Israelite people took an arduous journey through the wilderness for 40 years. In that time, God made a covenant with them. The Lord came down upon Mount Sinai, and Moses went up. Moses returned with the Covenant Code, a series of ritual and civil laws (Exodus 24:1-8).

Again, Moses went up the mountain to meet with the Lord. But this time, he returned with two tablets of stone containing the Ten Commandments, or the Decalogue, "written by God's finger" (31:18). But while Moses was away, Aaron had cast a golden calf that the people worshiped. When he saw it, Moses smashed the stone tablets in anger.

That's where this week's Focal Passage picks up. The Lord said to Moses, "Cut two stone tablets like the first ones. I'll write on these tablets the words that were on the first tablets, which you broke into pieces" (34:1). God again summoned Moses up Mount Sinai. But this time when Moses returned to the people, "the skin of his face shone brightly because he had been talking with God" (verse 29).

Exodus 34:29. The last time Moses came down from Mount Sinai with "two covenant tablets in his hand," he was met with rejection and chaos (Exodus 32:7-35). This time, Moses returned to acceptance and adulation. He had been reestablished as the Lord's spokesperson. This was symbolized by how "the skin of his face shone brightly because he had been talking with God" (34:29).

The verb for Moses' radiating face is used three times in our biblical passage (verses 29, 30, 35). But when this verb appears in Psalm 69:31, it means "horns." Confusion over this cognate connection led some early translators to mistakenly write, "His face was horned" (Exodus 34:29, Wycliffe Bible, Douay-Rheims Bible) and led Michelangelo to sculpt Moses with horns in the San Pietro in Vincoli, Rome.

It is difficult to define exactly what happened to the skin of Moses' face that made him shine so. Some scholars say he was transfigured in the manner of Jesus. Remember from the previous lesson "the appearance of [Jesus'] face changed" (Luke 9:29). But Matthew was the only Gospel writer to say Jesus' face actually "shone" (Matthew 17:2). Other scholars point to the similarity to "horns" described above, and they believe an exterior light (not touching his skin) radiated from him. But this is a minority opinion on the matter.

Similar imagery has been discovered in other writings from ancient Mesopotamia in which an awe-inspiring luminosity was a sign of divinity. In many of those non-biblical stories, a supernatural glow served as proof of a sovereign's legitimacy. In any case, Moses did not know his face was shining!

The verb tense implies Moses' face started shining when he was with God and kept shining when he came down the mountain. This day on which Moses brought the new covenant tablets from Mount Sinai has been memorialized in Judaism as the Day of Atonement, or Yom Kippur, the holiest day of the Jewish year.

Verse 30. When Aaron and the Israelites (literally, "the sons of Israel") saw Moses, their reaction was fear. Perhaps they were reminded of the powerful signs of the Lord's presence from Chapters 19–20 and 24, when "there was thunder, lightning, and a thick cloud on the mountain, and a very loud blast of a horn. All the people in the camp shook with fear" (19:16). Of course, the thunder, lightning, and all the rest were designed to instill the fear of God in the Israelites.

The radiance of Moses' face and the fear of the people give prominence to Moses as the mediator of God's word to the community of faith. The Hebrew root word for "speak" occurs seven times in our Focal Passage. The people now knew Moses spoke for God. Not only that, but in some sense, Moses embodied the word from God. Perhaps that is why this time the Israelites did not rebel against Moses and God as they did in Chapter 32.

Later, Old Testament writers probably thought back to this event when they wrote blessings and poetry about God's face shining on the people. For example, take a look at the familiar benediction in Numbers 6:24-26. It includes the line, "The LORD make his face shine on you and be gracious to you" (Numbers 6:25). Also consider the repeated phrase, "Make your face shine so that we can be saved" in Psalm 80:3, 7, 19.

No one else in the Bible is said to radiate light, save Jesus at his Transfiguration (Lesson 7). But when Moses appeared with Jesus on the Mount of Transfiguration, only Jesus shined, signifying Jesus' prominence over Moses and Elijah.

Verse 31. Notice Moses called Aaron and the leaders of Israel closer. This is similar to how the Lord had commanded Moses to ascend the mountain and approach the meeting place with the Lord. The Lord warned against letting anyone else up the mountain (save for the possible accompaniment of Joshua in Exodus 24:13). Thus, Aaron and the elders did not approach Moses on their own.

We remember Aaron as the high priest and as Moses' older brother. Since Moses had complained he was not an effective speaker, God gave him Aaron to assist him (Exodus 4:13-16). Famously, it was Aaron who consented to make for the Israelites a golden calf when Moses was away on Mount Sinai (32:2-4). When Moses confronted him, Aaron blamed the people (32:21-25).

Despite his leadership in the golden calf incident, Aaron remained Moses' trusted assistant. Like Moses, Aaron died outside the Promised Land (Deuteronomy 32:50). Later in Israel, Aaron was remembered as the model high priest and his families were exalted above other Levite families (Numbers 3:5-10). We do not know exactly what Moses told "Aaron and all the leaders of the community" (Exodus 34:31), but in the next verse "all the Israelites came near as well" (verse 32).

Verse 32. Moses did not bid the rest of the Israelites to come to him as he did "Aaron and all the leaders of the community" (verse 31). But perhaps the rest of the Israelites came near when they saw Aaron and the leaders were not hurt by seeing God's glory when they approached the radiant Moses.

Moses began, then, to reveal to the people the revelation he had on Mount Sinai. In particular, the writer is referring to the commandments and instructions related to disloyalty in verses 10-27. It was in that context the Lord said, "I hereby make a covenant with you and with Israel" (verse 27). The larger context, then, is the broad frame of Chapters 32–34.

The Hebrew verb used here for "commanded" means "he made them responsible for" or "he gave into their charge" (34:32). This is revealing because it means the people were to be the keepers of the Lord's instructions, not just Moses himself.

The chapters following this one show how the people took up the Lord's commandments and instructions and proceeded to build the Tabernacle.

Verse 33. "When Moses finished speaking with them, he put a veil over his face." We aren't told exactly why Moses needed this veil. He wasn't commanded by the Lord to use it. His shining presence was awe-inspiring, but it turned out not to be dangerous to the people. They approached him without harm in verses 31-32.

It's safe to assume one reason Moses put on a veil was so he would not frighten the people (verse 30). Some have also wondered if Moses was trying to hold in the glow so it was not cheapened or trivialized. The fact that Moses continued to glow is a testament to the power of the Lord's presence as well as Moses' role as God's authoritative mouthpiece.

The Hebrew word we translate as "veil" appears only in this passage. It appears to derive from a root word that refers to a covering (as in the mantle or cloak of Genesis 49:11). Moses' veil was not a cultic mask because he did not use it to conceal his identity or to assume the persona of a deity. Quite the opposite.

The people could welcome the glow from Moses' skin because it was like a reversal of the golden calf incident of Exodus 32. Rather than focusing on an idol, they could be reminded that the Lord God went with them. It meant hope in the midst of disaster.

Verses 34-35. The removal of the veil did then serve as an indicator Moses was going into the presence of the Lord. It was not necessary for Moses to veil his face for the benefit of the people when he was in the Lord's presence because only Moses could be in the Lord's presence in that way.

We are told God's radiance continued to shine from his skin when he came from these encounters with the Lord. The people could see it. No doubt it inspired awe and possibly still fear in them. In any case, it was clear to them Moses had been in the Lord's presence.

The text is not clear exactly where Moses was when he was in "the LORD's presence" (verse 34). This could have been a reference to the Tabernacle (about to be built), the tent of meeting of Exodus 33:7-11, Mount Sinai, some other place, or some combination of the above.

Notice Moses would come out of the Lord's presence and then tell the Israelites what God had commanded. Then he would veil his face. Therefore, the veiling of Moses' face might have also symbolized to the people the words he spoke through the veil were his own, not necessarily a word from the Lord. In this way, the veil could have been for Moses' benefit, too.

Moses' glow anticipates the glory of the Lord that would dwell in the Tabernacle and later the Temple. As we read in Exodus 40:34 and following, "The LORD's glorious presence filled the dwelling." A cloud over the dwelling by day and lightning in the dwelling at night indicated the Lord's presence with the people. No longer did the people need to wait while Moses spent 40 days and nights with God on Mount Sinai.

2 Corinthians 3:7-18. Paul referenced Moses' face when he wrote to the Christians in Corinth (2 Corinthians 3:7). He was trying to cement their relation to him and increase his authority in their eyes. So he employed a rhetorical strategy of comparison, first to Moses and our Focal Passage and second to Jeremiah's new covenant promise in Jeremiah 31:31-34.

In the comparison to Moses, Paul said, "The Israelites couldn't look for long at Moses' face because his face was shining with glory, even though it was a fading glory. Won't the ministry of the Spirit be much more glorious?" (2 Corinthians 3:7-8). The glory of Jesus Christ, he said, will not fade, but last.

In 2 Corinthians 3:12-18, Paul proclaimed we have hope and should thus act with confidence. He contrasted that with Moses, "who used to put a veil over his face so that the Israelites couldn't watch the end of what was fading away" (verse 13). Furthermore, he said, "Whenever Moses is read, a veil lies over their hearts" (verse 15). It is important to note this was Paul's particular interpretation of why Moses wore a veil. Nothing in the Exodus 34:29-35 account refers to a fading of glory from Moses' face.

But what Paul wanted to emphasize is "all of us" can now look at the glory of the Lord with "unveiled faces" when we look at the Spirit (2 Corinthians 3:18). Not only that, but "we are being transformed into that same image from one degree of glory to the next degree of glory" (verse 18).

For Paul, Jesus Christ is the reflection of God that Christians can see with an unveiled face. Believers can thus have access to God through Jesus Christ. Such access will transform them.

Reflect

In preparing to teach this lesson, keep in mind what we have learned thus far in this unit about the awe of God. You may want to remind class members about the previous lessons: Psalm 19 and the wonder of creation; Isaiah's call story and vision of God filling the Temple; and the Transfiguration of Jesus.

Remember, our God is a hidden and revealed God, but more hidden than revealed. But God graciously lets the divine glory seep out into our world. And even the small fraction of God's glory we see is more than enough to change us and our world. Look what a difference it made in (and on!) Moses and the Israelites in the Focal Passage for this lesson.

Your class members will come to your group time from busy lives. Perhaps their calendars are over-programmed. They may be spreading themselves thin between their many commitments. And all the while, they may be missing glimpses of the glory of God around them.

Let it be our goal this week to impress upon them God's glory is indeed around us if we have "eyes to see," as Jesus so often said. Think about what a difference it will make in their lives if they see God's glory in the faces of those around them! Imagine what awe they will experience!

If you have the *Adult Bible Studies* DVD, consider when you want your group to view the segment related to this lesson as you guide discussion around the text.

Begin by saying: ***Our lives are busy. We seldom have opportunity to stop and smell the roses, much less to look for God's glory on the faces of others. But think of someone in your life who just seems to radiate God's presence and glory. Picture them in your mind. Can you describe that person to the class?***

Class members will likely recall someone with whom they have had a personal relationship (a grandparent, parent, spouse, child, best friend, teacher, pastor). Explore with them what made that person radiate the glory of God. Ask: ***Were they especially caring? Strong in their faith? Did they pray a lot? What made them special?***

After some time of interpersonal sharing, reintroduce them to Moses. I say "reintroduce," because they likely all have visions of Moses in their minds (and some probably look a lot like Charlton Heston). Recall how Moses led God's people out of Egypt and to the Promised Land. But the people rebelled against God in the wilderness. Nevertheless, God made a new covenant with them.

Before you read the Focal Passage, review "A Little Context" in the student book, and read aloud Exodus 34:1-9 for context. God gave the people new tablets of stone with God's law written on them.

Next, ask volunteers to read aloud Exodus 34:29-35. Moses reflected God's glory from his encounter with God on Mount Sinai. Moses did not know he was glowing, but the people surely noticed. They were afraid. Ask: ***How do you think you would have reacted if you had been there and seen Moses' shining face?***

Next, point out how Aaron, the leaders of Israel, and the rest of the people reacted. After Moses called Aaron and the "leaders of the community" (verse 31) to him, the people saw they could encounter this reflection of the glory of God and still live. Remind the class the Hebrew belief was that you could not see God and live.

Moses' shining face was a reflection of the glory of God. Ask someone to read aloud Exodus 33:19-23, which describes how God put Moses in the gap of a rock, held a hand over Moses to shield him, and passed by so Moses saw only God's back. This could have been the moment Moses' face began to glow.

Then, ask class members to think of a time when they have had a mountaintop experience with the Lord. Ask: ***How was God's glory made known to you? How did it feel to have special time with God?***

As the teacher, you may want to think ahead of time of your own mountaintop experiences to share as examples. It may have been some time since your class members have felt God's presence in a rich way. Try to think of an example from your own life that is relatable. For example, maybe you were a youth at a Christian summer camp, or perhaps you think of many God-moments instead of one singular moment. Were your more powerful spiritual experiences in the presence of someone who radiated God's love for you?

Ask class members to respond to these questions from the student book: ***When have you seen something that affirmed God's presence with you? What did you see, and how did it affect your understanding of God?***

Be sure to leave time for discussion about Moses' veil. Refer to "The Veil" in the student book as you lead the class to consider the veil and its significance. As you learned in "Inspect," Moses did not use the veil to protect the people from his radiance. Quite the opposite. He removed it when he spoke with God and when he came out to speak to the people on God's behalf. But Moses did put on the veil when he was not speaking with or for God.

Some wonder if the veil helped the people distinguish between whether he was speaking for God or for himself. Others have theorized the veil was as much for Moses' benefit as for the people's. If class members are curious about the reason(s) for Moses' veil, feel free to share these theories. Maybe they have alternative theories to propose. Note the biblical writer says Moses wore the veil when he was not speaking with God or telling the people what God said. Ask: **Why do you think Moses wore the veil?**

Suggest, as noted in "Connect," that God is hidden and revealed but also more hidden than revealed. Explain it could have been Moses wanted to be judicious and conservative with his shining skin. Maybe he didn't want the people to get too used to seeing the glory of God reflecting on him. Ask: **Can you remember a time when you felt that the presence or power of God was so special that you wanted to keep it under a "veil"?**

I can recall a time or two when I experienced God's power in a way that was so special I wanted to just keep it to myself for awhile. I wasn't trying to be selfish, and I wasn't ashamed at all. It was just such a powerful and holy God-sighting that it took me a while to be able to talk about it. It happened when I was a student chaplain on call at the neonatal intensive care unit at the university hospital.

People who work on the front lines of life and death (medical professionals, soldiers on the battlefield, police, firefighters, and many others) experience moments that are difficult to talk about, but not always because they are bad moments. Sometimes they find it difficult to talk about holy moments because they are so holy. Maybe they can relate to Moses' practice of putting a veil over God's glory radiating from him.

Explain that whether we encounter God's glory in our own mountaintop experience or whether we see God's radiance in someone else, it is amazing to think God would let us see the divine light at all. Even more amazing is the idea we could, by the grace of God, show forth God's light in the world ourselves!

Close by praying together the prayer at the end of the lesson in the student book: **Dear God, we thank you that you do not hide yourself from us and that you know us and want us to know you. Expose the areas of our lives that need your forgiveness. Help us to listen to you more closely and walk with you more faithfully; in Jesus' name we pray. Amen.**

Then offer this benediction to the class:

"The Lord make his face shine on you and be gracious to you" (Numbers 6:25).

January 30 | Lesson 9

Joining the Choir of Angels

Focal Passages
Revelation 19:1-10

Background Text
Same

Purpose
To acknowledge only God is worthy of our worship

Revelation 19:1-10
¹After this I heard what sounded like a huge crowd in heaven. They said, "Hallelujah! The salvation and glory and power of our God!
²His judgments are true and just,
　because he judged the great prostitute,
　　who ruined the earth by her whoring,
　　and he exacted the penalty for the blood of his servants
　　　from her hand."
³Then they said a second time,
"Hallelujah! Smoke goes up from her forever and always."
⁴The twenty-four elders and the four living creatures fell down and worshipped God, who is seated on the throne, and they said, "Amen. Hallelujah!"
⁵Then a voice went out from the throne and said,
"Praise our God, all you his servants,
　and you who fear him, both small and great."
⁶And I heard something that sounded like a huge crowd, like rushing water and powerful thunder. They said,
"Hallelujah! The Lord our God, the Almighty,
　exercised his royal power!
⁷Let us rejoice and celebrate, and give him the glory,
　for the wedding day of the Lamb has come,
　and his bride has made herself ready.
⁸She was given fine, pure white linen to wear,
　for the fine linen is the saints' acts of justice."
⁹Then the angel said to me, "Write this: Favored are those who have been invited to the wedding banquet of the Lamb." He

said to me, "These are the true words of God." **¹⁰**Then I fell at his feet to worship him. But he said, "Don't do that! I'm a servant just like you and your brothers and sisters who hold firmly to the witness of Jesus. Worship God! The witness of Jesus is the spirit of prophecy!"

Key Verse: "Then I fell at his feet to worship him. But he said, 'Don't do that! I'm a servant just like you and your brothers and sisters who hold firmly to the witness of Jesus. Worship God! The witness of Jesus is the spirit of prophecy!'" (Revelation 19:10).

Connect

This might seem like a strange time of year to sing Handel's "Hallelujah Chorus," but it would be entirely appropriate because the text for this lesson is the great "Hallelujah Chorus" of the Book of Revelation! The previous chapter describes the fall of the great city of Babylon. The people of God were summoned to leave (Revelation 18:4-8). Various parties who had interests (economic, political, and so forth) in the success of the evil Babylon sang a funeral dirge (18:9-19).

John, the author of the Book of Revelation, then heard a "huge crowd" (19:1) that seemed to grow larger and louder (verse 6). Over and over again, they declared, "Hallelujah!" Most of our Focal Passage is their song. The conclusion (verses 9-10) contains John's reaction and news of a great "wedding banquet of the Lamb."

The Book of Revelation is apocalyptic literature. Apocalyptic literature is characterized by the author's image-rich visualizations meant to reveal things previously unknown.

Typically, apocalyptic writings are about the social, political, economic, and religious times in which they are written. The author takes a position of defense of God and God's plans against various powers (governments, rulers, authorities, for example) that are portrayed as the enemy or enemies of God. As in the Book of Revelation, God and God's forces defeat the powers and enemies.

To communities undergoing persecution, apocalyptic literature gave (and still gives) hope that God will one day have God's way with the world. In other words, no matter what adversity God's people face, stories like those in the Book of Revelation tell them God wins.

That is what our Focal Passage says: God wins! In typical apocalyptic fashion, the scene of God's triumph is rather surreal and fantastic, invoking a sense of wonder. New Babylon has been destroyed (18:1-8). A great prostitute who sat upon a scarlet beast (17:1-18) has been judged (19:2). Christ defeats the beast who, along with a false prophet, is thrown into the "fiery lake that burns with sulfur" (verse 20).

All of this leaves readers rocked back on our heels, in awe at the power of Christ to defeat evil in its real-world and supernatural forms. In particular, this text is a listening-in on a "huge crowd in heaven" (verse 1) as they sing their many hallelujahs.

In this unit, we have been studying passages that are awe-inspiring. We started with a psalm about creation (Lesson 5), journeyed to the days of the prophets (Lesson 6), climbed the Mount of Transfiguration with Jesus and three disciples (Lesson 7), and looked upon Moses' shining face (Lesson 8). It is fitting, then, our last lesson takes us to a vision of a future in which God's glory is fully and finally revealed.

Like John, our eyes grow wide at the splendor of God's triumph over evil. We find ourselves ready to fall down and worship. Our hearts sing with the heavenly chorus, "Hallelujah!"

This text is a gift because we spend so much of our days running about fretting about everyday matters. But John's revelation tells us God will triumph over all evil!

Hallelujah! Hallelujah! Amen!

Inspect

Revelation 19:1-8. Most of our Focal Passage is a hymn. Notice how the editors of your Bible probably indented verses 1-8 to look like poetry.

Biblical poetry is often divided into strophes (pronounced STROW-feez). The first strophe, verses 1-4, anticipates the judgment of the "great prostitute" (verse 2). The second strophe, verses 5-8, anticipates the wedding of the Lamb (Jesus) and his bride (the church).

Revelation 19:1. John, the narrator, said that he heard (not saw) "a huge crowd." Other translations say, "a great multitude" (NRSV, NIV). (It might be interesting to explore which phraseology members of your class prefer and why.) As they were told to do in Revelation 18:20, these "saints, apostles, and prophets" rejoiced over the fall of Babylon.

The crowd said, "Hallelujah!" which is a Greek transliteration of the Hebrew for "praise Yahweh" and can also be written "Allelujah!" Surprisingly, the four times the word "Hallelujah!" appears here in Revelation 19:1-6 are the only times the word appears in the New Testament.

This "Hallelujah Chorus" stands in stark contrast to the dirges of the kings, merchants, and seafarers who lost their economic power with the fall of Babylon (Revelation 18:9-19). The "Hallelujah!" is followed by "salvation and glory and power of our God!" (19:1). Just as an angel taunted Babylon in 18:2-3, now a huge crowd of heavenly beings declared God's victory as an established fact (as they did in 7:10, 11:15, and 12:10).

Verse 2. The heavenly crowd explained why they ascribed "salvation and glory and power" to God (verse 1). First, it was because "his judgments are true and just" (verse 2). This is a general statement about the nature of God. God has shown favor to God's servants by destroying those who destroy the earth (11:18).

Second, it was because the great prostitute "ruined the earth by her whoring" (19:2). This is a more specific charge that was leveled against her. The charge was the earth had been ruined by immorality, false worship, and brutality. This was a challenge to the Roman emphasis on virtue and good fortunes. Rome had corrupted the servants of God.

Finally, John heard the huge crowd say the great prostitute shed the blood of God's servants. The great prostitute had the blood of God's servants on her hands. That is why God "exacted the penalty for the blood of his servants from her hand" (19:2).

Since God is by nature absolutely just, evil must be punished. The crowd was certain God would avenge those who gave their lives for their faith. Other translations use the word "avenge," saying, "He has avenged on her the blood of his servants" (NRSV). The verb "to avenge" occurs only here and in Revelation 6:10, in which the martyrs cry out, "Sovereign Lord, holy and true, how long will it be before you judge and avenge our blood on the inhabitants of the earth?" (NRSV).

There is also an allusion here to 2 Kings 9:7, in which it is prophesied the Lord will "take revenge for the violence done by Jezebel to my servants the prophets and to all the Lord's servants."

Verse 3. The "huge crowd" (verse 1) returned to the "Hallelujah!" as "smoke goes up from her forever and always" (verse 3). This, too, is an allusion: In Isaiah 34:10, a prophecy against Edom says, "Its smoke will go up forever." We also read in the Gospels the fires of judgment in hell will burn forever (Matthew 18:8; 25:41; Mark 9:43, 48).

So the smoke must be going up from Babylon after its fiery destruction in Revelation 18:9, 18. This prompted the rejoicing of the multitudes and the finality of God's judgment (also Revelation 14:11). Babylon's smoke is in contrast to other smoke in Revelation like the smoke of incense, the prayers of the saints (8:4), and the smoke from God's glory that filled the Temple (15:8).

Verse 4. The 24 elders (4:4) and the four living creatures (4:6) will be familiar to those who studied Lesson 4 a few weeks ago. Just as they did in Revelation 4:10 and 5:14, here too they fell prostrate before God. Now John heard these elders and creatures repeat the "Hallelujah!" joined by the "Amen," which means "may it be so." The amen had a concluding function because a new voice was about to speak in verse 5.

Verse 5. The new voice came from the throne. One might assume the voice from the throne would be the voice of God. But the voice spoke about God in the third person.

Some commentators believe the voice from the throne was one of the 24 elders or one of the four creatures. Others wonder if the voice came from Christ, the Lamb. But in Revelation, Christ doesn't call for more praise. Christ receives praise. And others have a theory the speaker was an angel of the throne or the throne itself, but those theories are difficult to substantiate.

Even if we can't identify the speaker exactly, the point is another voice joined all the others. This voice from the throne must have significant divine authority to speak from such a centralized location in the heavenly court.

What did the throne-voice say? "Praise our God, all you his servants, and you who fear him, both small and great." This summons was directed to those on earth in contrast to the previous ones that had been directed to those who dwell in heaven. One can see a similar pattern in Psalm 148:1-6 and then in Psalm 148:7-14.

The voice from the throne summoned the voices like a choir director calling for more singers. These singers should sing out whether they are small or great, literally meaning "small ones" or "great ones," those of every station in life (Revelation 13:16).

Verse 6. Revelation 19 begins with "what sounded like a huge crowd in heaven" (verse 1), and now John reports he heard "something that sounded like a huge crowd" (verse 6). The phrase "sounded like" or "something that sounded like" may indicate the two crowds were different. John was a little uncertain about what he heard because he did not also see the crowd.

John also said it sounded "like rushing water and powerful thunder" (verse 6). These last two metaphors emphasize the loudness of the sound heard, perhaps a greater sound than that of verse 1.

The crowd, sea, and thunder were together singing another "Hallelujah!" But this time a reason is given for their exclamation: "The Lord our God, the Almighty, exercised his royal power" (verse 6)! In the great arc of the Book of Revelation, in the cosmic battle between God and Babylon, God has begun to reign!

The verb "to reign" is applied to God here and in Revelation 11:15 and 11:17. This is important because from John's perspective, God's sovereignty had not been obvious. Christians had languished under the oppressive powers of Rome, sometimes wondering if God was still in charge. John's vision gave them assurance and hope.

Verse 7. Revelation's "Hallelujah Chorus" continued with another call to praise from the "huge crowd" (verse 6). All who were listening were called to "rejoice and celebrate" (verse 7). The only other place where these two verbs appear together in the New Testament is in Matthew 5:12, the Beatitudes, where Jesus says his followers should "be full of joy and be glad" when they are insulted or harassed because "you have a great reward in heaven."

According to Revelation, the reward is a great wedding feast in which the Lamb and his bride are united. "The wedding day of the Lamb has come, and his bride has made herself ready" (verse 7). You've heard of the "wedding of the century." This is the wedding of all time, and this is the wedding invitation!

Christ is the Lamb, the bridegroom. The people of God are the bride. According to Jewish custom, until the time the bride is presented to her husband, she is expected to maintain her purity and faithfulness to her one husband. So in 2 Corinthians 11:2, for example, we read how Paul wished to betroth the church to Christ "as an innocent virgin." Ephesians 5:25-32 takes the metaphor further by saying the appropriate relationship between the husband and wife is the self-sacrificial love Jesus showed for the church. And we can't leave out the parable of the ten virgins in Matthew 25:1-13.

The expectation of the moment is heightened because the Lamb's bride "has made herself ready" (Revelation 19:7)! Class members who have been married may recall how excited they were right before the wedding.

Verse 8. We are now told how the bride, the church, has been made ready for the bridegroom. There is no mention of "something borrowed, something blue." Rather, she has been given "fine, pure white linen." John's first readers would have known this was suitable for the bride (Ezekiel 16:10).

The white linen is similar to the white robes of Revelation 3:5 in that it signifies purity and holiness. This is in contrast to the stains of sin which make one unclean (Revelation 3:4). In a similar way, the bride is in contrast to the great prostitute who "wore purple and scarlet clothing, and she glittered with gold and jewels and pearls" (Revelation 17:4).

Most Bibles treat Revelation 19:8 as the end of the "Hallelujah Chorus" that started in verse 6. But it also sounds as if John was giving some background information as an aside, for he tells us, "The fine linen is the saints' acts of justice" (verse 8). He has already told us our robes would need to be washed in the blood of the Lamb. This will give us access to the New Jerusalem (22:14). The martyrs will have already received their white robes (6:11).

Verse 9. The "Hallelujah Choruses" are concluded. John is speaking here, and he has been approached by "the angel," which is probably the bowl angel of 17:1. As in so many other places, John is instructed to "write this" (19:9).

The message of the angel is those who have been invited to the wedding banquet are favored or blessed. This is the fourth of seven such beatitudes in Revelation. It is similar to Luke 14:15, in which a dinner guest hears Jesus' remarks and says, "Happy are those who will feast in God's kingdom."

The wedding banquet of the Lamb is a triumphant, celebratory affair. It is a singular eschatological event found only in Revelation. And it is certainly not to be confused with the gory banquet in Revelation 19:17-21, in which the birds will feast on the corpses of the enemies of the white horse rider! No, the wedding banquet is akin to the Messianic feast Jesus referred to in verses such as Matthew 8:11 and Luke 22:30.

Verse 9 ends with one more word from the angel: "These are the true words of God." This is similar to the language we find in the pastoral epistles such as, "This saying is reliable and deserves full acceptance" (1 Timothy 1:15; also 3:1, 4:9; 2 Timothy 2:11; Titus 3:8). It serves as an amen.

Verse 10. John was so overwhelmed he felt the urge to prostrate himself in worship. The angel was the giver of these revelations, so John fell down before the angel. We've seen characters in our Bible bow down to the messenger before (for example, Daniel 2:46; Acts 10:25).

But the angel messenger corrected John, exclaiming, "Don't do that!" (Revelation 19:10). The angel was no god, but rather "a servant just like you and your brothers and sisters" (verse 10). We've heard this kind of conversation before in the Bible.

One example comes from Genesis 50:19, in which Joseph's brothers bowed down before him. But Joseph refused their worship, saying, "Don't be afraid. Am I God?" Another example comes from Acts 14:15. Barnabas and Paul rejected the worship of the people of Lystra: "People, what are you doing? We are humans too, just like you!"

Perhaps the most striking parallel to Revelation 19:9-10 comes just a few chapters later in this same book. Look at Revelation 22:8-9. There, you'll find an almost identical chain of events: John fell down and worshiped the angel, and the angel redirected John's worship to God.

The angel added a final word about the witness of Jesus and the spirit of prophecy. The witness of Jesus has a double meaning in the Greek. It could mean the witness that comes from Jesus, that is, what he said and did in the past. Or it could also mean the witness of Jesus, that is, what others have said concerning Jesus.

The "spirit of prophecy" can also have more than one meaning (19:10). It can refer to how God's Spirit communicates the prophecy, inspires the prophecy, or the inspired state in which John received the visions.

Reflect

This seems like a great occasion for a class party! Remember when you were in elementary school and you looked forward to the class party? Perhaps there was pizza for lunch or ice cream for dessert. Well, adults enjoy a good class party, too!

A party is appropriate because a great celebration is the theme of our Focal Passage. So if you can, decorate your meeting space with streamers, blow up some balloons, and do other things that suggest a party atmosphere. In that way, you will be helping set the context for this lesson, and you will certainly have class members' attention and imagination!

For your party music, I suggest a recording of Handel's "Hallelujah Chorus" from his "Messiah." Multiple recordings licensed for free public use are available by an Internet search. You may have class members who are in the church choir and some who have sung the "Hallelujah Chorus."

Also ahead of time, gather hymnals for class members to use.

Once you have set the party atmosphere and enjoyed surprising class members, show the segment of the *Adult Bible Studies* DVD related to this lesson if you have it. Then say: ***This week we are studying John's vision of a great party in heaven. The forces of evil, represented by Babylon, have fallen. Now John hears a great "Hallelujah Chorus."***

Refer to the opening paragraphs of the lesson in the student book that describe Handel's "Hallelujah Chorus," and talk about the role of music in our worship. Then review "Reason to Rejoice?" in the student book to further set the stage for the Focal Passage.

Next, ask volunteers to read aloud Revelation 19:1-8. Note verses 1-8 contain a series of stanzas to this Hallelujah chorus. Verses 1 and 2 are the first stanza. They burst forth with praise and state two reasons for the praise: "He judged the great prostitute, who ruined the earth by her whoring," and "he exacted the penalty for the blood of his servants from her hand" (verse 2).

Verse 3 might be considered another stanza, or at least a refrain, in which the same "huge crowd in heaven" (verse 1) is praising God.

Note in the first three verses we hear the initial song of praise. Ask: ***What great praise hymns or songs do you love? What lyrics speak for your heart?***

Distribute hymnals among class members so they can look up favorites and read praise-filled lyrics to the class. Note that verse 4 is not so much a stanza in the Hallelujah chorus as it is a call-back to an earlier part of Revelation. Remind students of the lesson from December 26 that was also from Revelation by saying: ***A few weeks ago, right after Christmas Day, we studied Revelation 3:20–4:11. There, we read about the 24 elders and the four living creatures. Here they are again in Revelation 19:4!***

Ask class members what they remember from that lesson. Recall that Revelation is a book full of vivid apocalyptic imagery. Readers find themselves cheering for God's side as the story unfolds. Ask: ***How does it make you feel to see these same "characters" come back to join the Hallelujah chorus?***

Point out verse 5 is like another stanza in the chorus. A voice comes from the throne. But we should not assume it is the voice of God or Jesus (see "Inspect"). It is another heavenly voice that praises God. It's as if members of the heavenly congregation are shouting out their praise. Ask: ***Have you ever wanted to shout "Amen" or "Hallelujah" in worship? Does something hold you back? Why or why not?***

Point out the last stanza of this Hallelujah chorus comes in verses 6-8, which are similar to verses 1-2. But this time, John said he heard "a huge crowd, like rushing water and powerful thunder" (verse 6). This represents a great crescendo from the "huge crowd" of verse 1.

You might draw an (albeit inadequate) analogy to listening to music or a movie over a massive high-fidelity sound system. What a difference it makes to the listener's experience!

We can hardly begin to imagine what this powerfully loud sound must have been like for John.

In verse 7, the chorus introduces a subject that will carry over to verse 9: the wedding feast of the Lamb. This is a future joining together of the Lamb/bridegroom (who is Jesus Christ) with his bride (who is the faithful church). "His bride has made herself ready" by her faithfulness (verse 7). See this verse in "Inspect" for more information.

Say: *In verse 7, we are told about a wedding day between Jesus and the faithful church. In verse 9, we will receive our invitation to the wedding banquet.* Ask: *What do you love about a wedding? How does wedding imagery help you celebrate what God has done in bringing together Jesus and the faithful church?*

Before you conclude, read aloud verses 9 and 10. They are not part of this "Hallelujah Chorus" as such, but they are an aside between the angel and John. As in so many other places in Revelation, the angel said, "Write this" (verse 9). Just as it is important John saw these visions, it was important he write them down for current and future generations of Christians to find inspiration and hope.

Say: *The angel told John to write all this down. If he had not written it down, we might not be reading it now. We're reminded of the importance of the Word of God and the role of those who wrote it down for us.*

John had just had a vision of the fall of Babylon. He watched the forces of domination and evil succumb to the overwhelming power of God and God's agents. After all John had seen, he felt the instinctual need to fall down and worship! Who can blame him?

Perhaps class members can think of a time when they felt so grateful they wanted to fall to their needs and give thanks. Consider how you might ask them for an example. But be aware such a story might be too personal for some of them to talk about. You might need to search your memory for your own example and be prepared to offer it first.

Note John worshiped the wrong entity! The angel told him, "Don't do that!" and we can imagine the angel helping John to his feet (Revelation 19:10). John should have been worshiping the Lamb, the Lord Jesus. It's an understandable mistake, but a symbolic one, too.

Stress that John was so overwhelmed with awe he fell down to worship, but he fell down before the angel. Say: *If we're not careful, we can misdirect our worship even to good things. Can you think of an example where this can happen?* (*Examples you might offer in the course of discussion include a religious leader, an institutional church, or a physical object in the worship space. Even the Bible itself can become an object of misdirected worship. Our worship should be directed to God.*)

The angel even stated it plainly to John: "Worship God!" (verse 10)! This is what our lesson is all about: God's awe-inspiring great triumph over Babylon and all that Babylon represents. We are caught up in the visions, sounds, and experiences of John.

Like the heavenly choruses, we say, "Hallelujah!" We anticipate the great banquet with our own party, and we live in the present as those who know how the story will end. As the angel told John, so we declare, "These are the true words of God" (verse 9).

Close by reminding class members of the spiritual practice the lessons in this unit have encouraged. Point out the suggestions for engaging this practice at the end of the lesson in the student book. Then close by praying together the prayer at the end of the lesson in the student book: **Dear God, help us recognize your power and authority and sense your presence and protection, even and especially when circumstances around us cause us to doubt. Remind us that you alone are worthy of our worship; in Jesus' name. Amen.**

Unit 3: Introduction

Show and Tell

Throughout this quarter, our lessons have shown us how we can participate with God. First, we participated by waiting during Advent and Christmas (Unit 1). Then we participated in wonder by witnessing some of the most amazing, eye-opening accounts of the Bible (Unit 2). We close out the quarter by better understanding how we participate in God's work by what we say and what we do.

Our lessons in Unit 3 are about God's gracious act of incorporating us into God's mighty works of salvation. Does God need us to accomplish the redemptive work? No, but I like to believe God has seen what joy we can have when we participate in God's work.

So in choosing the texts for the lessons in this unit, the editors asked, "What Scripture passages remind us we are included in God's work in the world?" We must start, as we do, with the law God gave through Moses and the lawgivers of ancient Israel. All of the Law is based on one great commandment: "Love the LORD your God with all your heart, all your being, and all your strength" (Deuteronomy 6:5). This is the first commandment we will study in Lesson 10.

In Matthew and Luke, Jesus was asked what the greatest commandment is, and he answered by quoting Deuteronomy 6:5 and by adding Leviticus 19:18, which says, "Love your neighbor as yourself." On these two, Jesus said, the rest of the Law and the Prophets depend (Matthew 22:40).

It would be enough that we would love God and neighbor because God told us to, but there is an added dimension: When we follow Jesus' ways, we are like a light to the world. Jesus told us as much in Matthew 5:14-16, the text for Lesson 11. Yes, Jesus did say he is the Light of the world in John 8:12, but that was in a different context.

In the nine verses that make up Lesson 12, we will encounter three emphases: (1) being quick to listen and slow to speak (James 1:19-21), (2) being doers of the word and not hearers only (verses 22-25), and (3) the nature of true devotion (verses 26-27).

Finally, Unit 3 brings us to the Great Commission in Lesson 13. It is the culmination of our whole quarter's emphasis on engagement with God. The Great Commission of Matthew 28:16-20 is supremely important because it is Jesus' final, detailed instructions to us before his departure from earthly ministry.

Of all the things Jesus said, taught, and did, he put before his disciples these final instructions: "Go and make disciples of all nations, baptizing them in the name of the Father and of the Son and of the Holy Spirit, teaching them to obey everything that I've commanded you" (Matthew 28:19-20). If the Great Commandments summed up the Law and the Prophets, the Great Commission sums up how we should go about loving God and neighbor.

What a great way to wrap up a unit on participating in God's work in the world! Jesus reminds us that his work is ongoing in us through the Holy Spirit. It doesn't just end with him. It only begins with him. And as his modern disciples, it is our joyous task to participate in God's work by making disciples of Jesus Christ!

The Tefillin, the Phylactery, and the Mezuzah

From Lesson 10, we know the *Shema*, Deuteronomy 6:4-5, is the centerpiece of daily evening and morning Jewish prayer services. Many parents in the Jewish faith say it with their children at bedtime, and Jews are encouraged to make the *Shema* their last words before death.

We also read in Deuteronomy 6:8-9 an observant Jew is to tie the *Shema* "on your hand as a sign. They should be on your forehead as a symbol. Write them on your house's doorframes and on your city's gates."

That's a lot of places to put these two verses of Scripture. But when we think about it, how many of us have words of Scripture in artwork on our walls at home? How many of us have an inspirational verse on our cellphone wallpaper or on a sticky note on the car dashboard or the refrigerator door?

Ancient Israelites knew just as well as we do that putting a Bible verse where you will see it again and again is key to making it part of your life. But a lot of us today may not realize how literally some Orthodox Jews take these instructions.

As you read in Lesson 10's "Inspect" for Deuteronomy 6:8 and 9, there has long been a practice of literally tying the *Shema* to one's hands and forehead as well as to one's doorpost and the city gates.

Tefillin or *phylacteries* are terms for small black leather boxes that contain scrolls of parchment from the Torah certain to include the *Shema*. The arm *teffillah* is placed on the upper arm, and the strap wrapped around the arm, hand and fingers. The head *tefillah* is placed above the forehead.

The *mezuzah* is a decorative case that contains a piece of parchment on which is written the *Shema* and a few other important verses of Torah.

Some Jewish homes have one *mezuzah* on the doorframe of the front door. Others put them on the doorframe of every "lived in" room of the house. Many observant Jews even have a qualified scribe check the parchment for defects at least twice every seven years.

February 6 | Lesson 10
The Greatest Commandments

Focal Passages
Deuteronomy 6:4-9; Matthew 22:34-40

Background Text
Same

Purpose
To renew our commitment to the Great Commandments

Deuteronomy 6:4-9
⁴Israel, listen! Our God is the LORD! Only the LORD!

⁵Love the LORD your God with all your heart, all your being, and all your strength. ⁶These words that I am commanding you today must always be on your minds. ⁷Recite them to your children. Talk about them when you are sitting around your house and when you are out and about, when you are lying down and when you are getting up. ⁸Tie them on your hand as a sign. They should be on your forehead as a symbol. ⁹Write them on your house's doorframes and on your city's gates.

Matthew 22:34-40
³⁴When the Pharisees heard that Jesus had left the Sadducees speechless, they met together. ³⁵One of them, a legal expert, tested him. ³⁶"Teacher, what is the greatest commandment in the Law?"

³⁷He replied, "*You must love the Lord your God with all your heart, with all your being, and with all your mind.* ³⁸This is the first and greatest commandment. ³⁹And the second is like it: *You must love your neighbor as you love yourself.* ⁴⁰All the Law and the Prophets depend on these two commands."

Key Verse: "He replied, You must love the Lord your God with all your heart, with all your being, and with all your mind. This is the first and greatest commandment" (Matthew 22:37-38).

Connect

Our family likes jigsaw puzzles. We usually have a puzzle under construction on a craft table. A big puzzle can even take over our dining room table. We enjoy being able to sit down, put some pieces in the right places, and leave it for the next person to work on.

Lately, however, we've learned not all puzzles are fun for us. One of my daughters and I started a daunting 1,500-piece puzzle, the largest we've ever tried. "We can do 1,000-piece puzzles," we said, "so this will be even more fun."

We were wrong! The puzzle difficulty level was so high the fun wore off quickly. The work went too slowly. We weren't getting the tiny moments of satisfaction of finding where a piece fit.

Following Jesus is difficult, too. At times it can be so difficult we feel overwhelmed. We might miss those tiny moments of satisfaction when things fit together well in our discipleship. We might even lose our joy.

What can we do? How can we be faithful in our discipleship when following Jesus can be so difficult? We can start by looking at today's texts in which God's Word distills "all the Law and the Prophets" (Matthew 22:40) down to two Great Commandments.

When pressed by a lawyer of the Pharisees to declare what is the greatest commandment of all, Jesus referenced Deuteronomy 6:5. "Love the LORD your God with all your heart, all your being, and all your strength." To that Jesus added a second commandment from Leviticus 19:18. *"You must love your neighbor as you love yourself"* (Matthew 22:39).

These words are a gift to us when we feel overwhelmed by the demands of discipleship. When we don't know what God would have us do, when we aren't sure how to make sense of a situation, when we feel directionless, we can center ourselves on these two Great Commandments to love God and neighbor.

The Great Commandments serve as a litmus test for our words, thoughts, and actions. We can ask ourselves, "Am I loving God with all my heart, all my being, and all my mind? Am I loving my neighbor as myself?"

The last four lessons this quarter follow the theme "Show and Tell." God has graciously given us an opportunity to be part of God's work in the world. We get a front-row seat!

But how shall we participate in God's work? This lesson doesn't seek to answer what we should do. Lessons 11, 12, and 13 will address that. This lesson challenges us to consider how we will participate in God's work. With what attitude? The *Shema* in Deuteronomy 6:4-9 and Jesus' restatement of the Great Commandments in Matthew 22:34-40 tell us how: with our whole being, with everything we are, and with everything we have.

As you move through these texts with your class, remember these Great Commandments are meant to help us understand and apply God's will in our lives, not to make life more difficult than it already is. Loving God and neighbor as we should is still difficult; but by God's grace, we have these two Great Commandments to guide us.

Inspect

Deuteronomy 6:4-9. If we had to pick a pivotal passage in all of Deuteronomy, it would be this one. Everything leading up to Chapter 6 has been a recounting of God's faithfulness to Israel. And everything following Chapter 6 is about how the Israelites should follow the commandments in 6:4-9.

Deuteronomy 6:1-3 signifies how important these laws will be for the Israelites: "Follow them carefully so that things will go well for you and so that you will continue to multiply exactly as the LORD, your ancestors' God, promised you, in a land full of milk and honey" (Deuteronomy 6:3).

Verses 4-9 have been traditionally credited to Moses. It begins with the *Shema* in verse 4. Then Moses spoke the Great Commandment: "Love the LORD your God with all your heart, all your being, and all your strength" (verse 5).

Deuteronomy 6:4. "Israel, listen! Our God is the LORD! Only the LORD!" has a place of great prominence in the Jewish faith. Known as the *Shema* (pronounced shu-MA), it is the centerpiece of daily evening and morning Jewish prayer services. Many parents in the Jewish faith say it with their children at bedtime, and believers are encouraged to make the *Shema* their last words before death.

Verse 4 is prominent in Christian worship liturgy, too. In the Catholic Liturgy of the Hours, it is recited in the Night Prayer (complines) on Saturday evening, and it appears in the Anglican *Book of Common Prayer*.

Even though the *Shema* is familiar, the Hebrew in verse 4 is complicated and permits variations in translation. But all of them say God is One, and Yahweh is Israel's unique God.

In the ancient Near East, different cities and cultures had their own gods. People traveling between cities and cultures would often pay their respects to the local gods whether they believed in them or not. But Israel's claim is they have the one true God. Israel's God is not a god among many other or competing gods.

Finally, notice the similarities between today's text and the beginning of the Ten Commandments in Deuteronomy 5:6-7. "You must have no other gods before me," is another way of saying the Lord is Israel's one and only God (5:7).

Verse 5. This verse begins with a command that is lost in some English translations. The first words should be, "You *shall* love" (NRSV; italics added). The idea of commanding a feeling like love may seem strange to us, but it was a familiar part of the Israelite Torah (Law).

The Torah assumes humans can cultivate the proper attitude toward the Lord through putting their love into action. Love of God is not just an emotional attachment. It is a command. Love is expressed in benevolent actions.

This runs both ways. When Deuteronomy describes God's love for humanity, it means a love expressed through God's actions as in Deuteronomy 10:18, in which God "enacts justice for orphans and widows, and he loves immigrants, giving them food and clothing."

Deuteronomy is actually the first book in the Torah (the first five books of our Old Testament) to speak of a loving God. The preceding four books emphasize reverence, traditionally referred to as the "fear of God." But Deuteronomy brings together the fear of God with the love of God (10:12; 13:4-5).

How shall we "love the LORD your God" (6:5)? Moses gave three ways:

1. *with all your heart*. The Hebrew word for "heart" refers to the interior of the body. It was thought of as the seat of thought, intention, and feeling. Later Greek notions of the mind did not come into play at this time, and we should not read them back into this ancient text.

2. *with all your being*. Many English translations use the word "soul" here. The ancient Hebrew word for "soul" referred to one's emotions, passions, and desires. Often, the words for "heart" and "soul" were used together to indicate the entirety of a person.

3. *with all your strength*. This means "exceedingly" and gives the previous commands the strongest possible emphasis. It has traditionally also had a monetary connotation, denoting you should show your love for God with your wealth. And strength also adds to the idea that love of God is not just an emotion, but it also requires benevolent action and self-discipline.

In all three exhortations, the emphasis is on the word "all." Just as the Lord is Israel's God alone, so must the Israelites dedicate all of themselves to the Lord.

Verse 6. The NRSV reads, "Keep these words that I am commanding you today in your heart." Moses spoke here as a teacher reminding the Israelites to internalize this Great Commandment, not just to have it "on your minds" (CEB).

Moses was bringing the people a command from the one and only Lord God (verse 4). It was not a suggestion or an idealized preference. It was a divine edict from sovereign to subjects.

"These words that I am commanding you today" refers not only to the Great Commandment, but also to all the Law and teachings in Deuteronomy. Thus Jewish religious practices often require the personal writing and recitation of large portions of the Law (as in the bar and bat mitzvah ceremonies).

Verse 7. This verse states "these words" (verse 6) should be recited to children, discussed around the house, from the time you wake up to the time you go to bed.

As previously mentioned, the *Shema* is often a bedtime prayer for Jewish children and parents. And as the Law should be talked about "when you are lying down and when you are getting up," so too is the *Shema* part of traditional Jewish evening and morning prayers.

English readers might have expected the verse to say, "When you are getting up and when you are laying down," as in "morning to evening." But the ancient Hebrew day began at sundown the day before.

Orally talking about the Law in one's household was the primary means of instruction in ancient Israel before the spread of literacy in the populace.

Verse 8. Another way the faithful Israelites were reminded of the Law was to tie it "on your hand as a sign" and "on your forehead as a symbol." Based on this verse, many Orthodox Jewish men today wear boxes with tiny copies of the *Shema* (plus three related texts) on their hands (*tefillin*) and on their foreheads (*phylactery*).

These boxes are constructed with precisely 12 stitches to represent the 12 tribes of Israel. They bind these boxes to their bodies with many straps as a literal interpretation of verse 8 that says, "Tie them on your hand." Reformed Jewish traditions view this command as more symbolic, meaning binding the law to your whole heart and life.

Verse 9. Just as small copies of the *Shema* are worn on hands and foreheads, many Jewish households today have a *mezuzah* (meaning "doorpost") by the door of their home. In ancient times, the *Shema* would even be written directly on their doorways. As they left home and returned home, the faithful would see the words of the *Shema* and be reminded of the Law.

The "city's gates" were a set of doors under a roofed structure that included several chambers and benches. Such an area functioned as a center of public activity. The *Shema* written in the city gates complex would be seen by all who entered and exited the city, Jews and alien visitors.

Matthew 22:34-40. We find the context of these words in Matthew 22:15-16 when "the Pharisees met together to find a way to trap Jesus in his words. They sent their disciples, along with the supporters of Herod, to him." Jesus was also questioned by the Sadducees on the same day (verse 23).

These interrogators posed three questions to Jesus to trap him: (1) a question about taxes in Matthew 22:16-22; (2) a question about resurrection in Matthew 22:23-33; and (3) a question about the Great Commandment in Matthew 22:34-40. Following their questions, Jesus posed one to them about "David's son" in Matthew 22:41-46. After they couldn't answer Jesus' question, Matthew says, "From that day forward nobody dared to ask him anything" (verse 46).

Matthew 22:34-40 was probably based on Mark 12:28-34. It has a parallel in Luke 10:25-28, in which it is followed by the parable of the good Samaritan (Luke 10:29-37).

Matthew 22:34. In Matthew 22:23-33, Jesus responds to a question from the Sadducees such that "when the crowd heard this, they were astonished at his teaching" (verse 33). This is what Matthew meant when he said, "The Pharisees heard that Jesus had left the Sadducees speechless" (verse 34).

Matthew's Greek word for "speechless" means "muzzled." It indicates they did not know what to say. So the Pharisees gathered together to discuss the matter so they might still "trap Jesus in his words" (verse 15). We do not know the content of their discussion because one of them starts questioning Jesus in verse 35.

Verse 35. Jesus' questioner is not named. We only know he was a "legal expert." The question he actually asked in verse 36 does not seem like a trick question. Nevertheless, Matthew tells us the lawyer meant to entrap Jesus.

Verse 36. Throughout Matthew 22, Jesus' questioners have used the polite form of address, "Teacher," even though they had been trying to trap him (verses 16, 24, 36).

The question put to Jesus was, "What is the greatest commandment in the Law?" As Gary Thompson notes in the student book, rabbis of that time found 613 different commandments in the Law. They regarded some as weightier than others. Rabbinic discussions and papers were (and still are) written about which ones are weighty and how to follow the Law in various hypothetical situations.

Perhaps the lawyer wanted to initiate such a discussion that he hoped would lead to a dispute between Jesus and the Pharisees. They hoped they might be able to damage Jesus' reputation in that subsequent dispute.

Verse 37. Perhaps Jesus' hearers expected him to quote one of the Ten Commandments. But in this verse, Jesus quotes Deuteronomy 6:5, part of the other Focal Passage for this lesson.

In Matthew's account, Jesus makes one change, however, by saying "with all your mind" rather than "all your strength" (Deuteronomy 6:5). Mark and Luke quote Jesus as saying both "mind" and "strength."

This change was probably due to the Hellenistic (Greek) Jewish tradition that had developed in Jesus' time. Most Greek philosophy divided the person into the body, mind, and soul. But the intention behind Jesus' words is the same: to love God with one's whole being.

Verse 38. Jesus had been asked which is the "greatest commandment" (verse 36), but he added that the *Shema* is the "first and greatest commandment" (verse 38). In Mark's version, the questioner asked what was the "first commandment" (Mark 12:28, NRSV). So Jesus' summary in this verse includes both "first and greatest" (Matthew 22:38).

Verse 39. Though the Pharisee lawyer asked only about "the greatest commandment" (verse 36), Jesus added a "second commandment" that is "like it" (verse 39). Alongside loving God, Jesus said, *"You must love your neighbor as you love yourself."* He was drawing from Leviticus 19:18, 34.

The Hebrew word for "neighbor" is somewhat elastic, but most Jewish interpreters of the time thought it referred to one's fellow Jew. Of course, Jesus upended that notion in Luke's parallel account when the legal expert asked,

"And who is my neighbor?" (Luke 10:29).

Jesus had already presented this commandment in Matthew 5:43 (partially) and 19:19. We can find a parallel sentiment in 1 John 4:20, which reads, "Those who say, 'I love God' and hate their brothers or sisters are liars." Likewise, James 2:8 states that the law to love your neighbor as yourself is "the royal law found in scripture."

Verse 40. These two commands are so important that Jesus said, "All the law and the prophets depend" on them. Remember, he was only asked about the Law. Jesus added the reference to the prophets. He had already said something similar in the Sermon on the Mount: "You should treat people in the same way that you want people to treat you; this is the Law and the Prophets" (Matthew 7:12).

Anyone who loves God and neighbor in such a way will not come up short in their religious faithfulness. By saying that all the Law and prophets "hang on" these (Matthew 22:40, NRSV), Jesus was saying that there is no need for other laws or hair-splitting. The commandments are all important, but only if we obey them out of love of God and neighbor.

Reflect

As you prepare to teach a lesson with a New Testament passage that is so largely based on an Old Testament passage, consider what approach you will take. Will you start with the Deuteronomy text and then move to the Matthew text? Or will you start with the Matthew text and then use the Deuteronomy text for context?

I know as a preacher of the gospel, if I'm not careful, I will fail to give the Old Testament its fair time in the spotlight. I don't believe I'm alone in that. For example, I don't own a "red-letter Bible," but I understand how they became popular. Christians want to find and read the words of Jesus.

So it is my advice that we not spend so much class time on Matthew that we make the *Shema* seem like an afterthought. After all, it was Jesus himself who told us it was the most important of the commandments! If it was that important to him, it ought to be just as important to us.

Another note as you begin your preparation: Don't forget the Purpose Statement of the lesson. These particular texts are so rich and so applicable to our lives we could have a wonderful time exploring and examining them and never get back around to our purpose in doing so: to participate in God's work.

As stated in "Connect," God has graciously given us an opportunity to be part of the divine work in the world. We get a front-row seat! Let's come back around to that at least one more time before class time is over.

If you have the *Adult Bible Studies* DVD, plan to show the segment related to this lesson when everyone arrives.

Then begin discussion by saying: ***Being a faithful Christian can be difficult. Do you ever feel overwhelmed by all the laws and*** *commandments in the Bible? Do you ever feel insufficient to the task of discipleship? In the texts for this lesson, the Bible distills all of God's teachings into two commandments: love God, and love your neighbor.*

Form two groups. Assign one group Deuteronomy 6:4-9. Assign the other group Matthew 22:34-40. Ask each group to read the assigned text together and be prepared to present key findings and take-aways to the other group. Refer them to "The *Shema*" and "Love Your Neighbor" in the student book.

You might also consider giving them photocopies of "Inspect." Ask each group to make notes about what they discover when they read their text closely. Explain you are looking for information on the content and the context of each passage. Ask them to consider: *What was happening when the passage was written? What makes that passage important in the Bible?*

Explain that these questions will help you start with a surface reading. It's too soon to get into application. Be sure the class understands Jesus was quoting from Deuteronomy 6 and Leviticus 19:18.

When you bring the two groups back together, call for a report from the Deuteronomy group first. Record their discoveries on a white board or a flipchart. Then call for a report from the Matthew group, and record their findings as well. Use "Inspect" to help the class draw the parallels between the passages.

Point out that Jesus quoted the *Shema*, the great commandment God gave the people through Moses. A lawyer from the Pharisees pressed him to name the greatest commandment. Jesus also added Leviticus 19:18, which says to love your neighbor as yourself. "All the Law and the Prophets depend on these two commands," he said (Matthew 22:40).

It is interesting Jesus was asked about one commandment but responded with two. Ask: *Why do you suppose he did that?* Here you are not looking for one particular answer. You are simply inviting class members into the text for deeper exploration. Welcome their attempts to tie the two commandments together. They are developing a sense of why these two were the most important to Jesus and beginning to think of them in their own lives.

Note, when Jesus brought up the second commandment to love your neighbor as yourself, he didn't say the second one was less important. He said it was "like" the first commandment (Matthew 22:39). The Greek word he used was *homoia* (pronounced ho-mo-EE-ah), as in *homogeneous* or *homonym*, meaning "of the same kind."

As we read in multiple places in 1 John, we cannot love God without loving our neighbor. "This commandment we have from him: Those who claim to love God ought to love their brother and sister also" (1 John 4:21). And as Jesus himself explained in Matthew 25:31-46, what we do (or don't do) for the least of Jesus' brothers or sisters, we do (or don't do) for him.

Stress that by bringing together two texts (Deuteronomy 6:5; Leviticus 19:18), Jesus asserted the principle of love applies equally to these two aspects of religious duty. Our attitude toward God is inseparable from our attitude toward neighbor. Now, help your class members come back around to the purpose of the lesson: to participate in God's works.

Say: *God has graciously given us an opportunity to participate in God's works. To that end, we hope to renew our commitment to the Great Commandments.* Ask: *What does it mean to you that God has given us these two Great Commandments?* Encourage class members to reflect on their personal experiences with these commandments. When are they difficult? When are they easy?

Suggest each of us at times might feel overwhelmed by Jesus' expectations of our discipleship. These two commandments are life-giving in their simplicity. If we start with them and obey them, then other aspects of following Jesus will fall into place.

Point out how interesting it is that our Matthew text came out of a Pharisaical attempt to trap Jesus! But Jesus turned that threat into an opportunity to teach his hearers what is most important. In Luke's account, Jesus even used this question to springboard into the parable of the good Samaritan (Luke 10:26-37).

In Matthew's telling of this encouter, Jesus' answer was satisfactory to the lawyer the Pharisees had sent. After they asked him one more question (about David's son) Jesus satisfied and even confounded his questioners. Matthew added, "From that day forward nobody dared to ask him anything" (Matthew 22:46). My teenaged children would call that a "mic drop" moment!

It is hard to live by Jesus' example. Sometimes we need to hear it in simple terms such as Jesus gave us in these two Great Commandments.

Encourage class members to recommit to using the Great Commandments as guides. Moses told the people to recite them to their children, talk about them, and put them where they would remember them (Deuteronomy 6:7-9). Let us also have "these words . . . always be on our minds" (verse 6).

Close class time by praying together the prayer at the end of the lesson in the student book: **Dear God, thank you for loving us with an everlasting, unconditional love. Teach us to love others as you have loved us. We are grateful for those who have shared your love with us. Teach us how to effectively share your love in word and deed; in Jesus' name. Amen.**

The Spiritual Practice of Testimony

The last four lessons this quarter center on the theme "Show and Tell." Quite naturally, then, the spiritual practice these lessons encourage is testimony in word and deed. Many people are uncomfortable with the idea of sharing their faith with others. Many have never done it. Some may feel guilty about this.

Even with pointed words from Jesus about going and telling and making disciples, some class members will feel neither compelled nor equipped to offer a faith testimony. What can you do to help? One way is to introduce resources to them that can increase their confidence and help them better understand that testimony is more than words. It is quite often most effective in deeds.

United Methodists have access to an often untapped storehouse of resources that can educate, motivate, and inspire believers to, among other things, share their faith: *umc.org*. In addition to articles, this site includes numerous videos and podcasts suitable for individual and group viewing/listening.

As you lead your class to study the biblical texts in Unit 3, spend personal time at this website. Select a video or a podcast to share with your class in conjunction with these Bible lessons. Make available to class members the website address so they can read, view, and listen on their own. Here are some suggestions:

- "Rethinking What We Mean When We Talk About Evangelism" (*umc.org/en/content/rethinking-what-we-mean-with-evangelism*)
- "Life Experience Creates the Best Witness of Faith" (*umc.org/en/content/life-experience-creates-the-best-witness-of-faith*)
- "Living Our Faith Daily" (*umc.org/en/content/get-your-spirit-in-shape-living-our-faith-daily*)
- "How a Church Shares Faith Where Faith Is Suspect" (*umc.org/en/content/how-a-church-shares-faith-where-faith-is-suspect-wsf*)

You may want to involve a couple of class members in researching articles, videos, and podcasts on this site and ask them to report back to the class with a list of helpful suggestions.

Jesus said, "You are the salt of the earth. But if salt loses its saltiness, how will it become salty again? It's good for nothing except to be thrown away and trampled under people's feet. You are the light of the world. A city on top of a hill can't be hidden. Neither do people light a lamp and put it under a basket. Instead, they put it on top of a lampstand, and it shines on all who are in the house. In the same way, let your light shine before people, so they can see the good things you do and praise your Father who is in heaven" (Matthew 5:13-16).

There are many ways we can be salt and light. As we live into Jesus' expectations of us, remember that we do not go alone. He goes with us, beside us, before us, and behind us, showing us what to do and telling us what to say.

February 13 | Lesson 11
Making God's Light Visible

Focal Passages
Matthew 5:14-16

Background Text
Matthew 5:1-16

Purpose
To explore how our actions make God's glory and love for the world evident

Matthew 5:14-16
¹⁴You are the light of the world. A city on top of a hill can't be hidden. ¹⁵Neither do people light a lamp and put it under a basket. Instead, they put it on top of a lampstand, and it shines on all who are in the house. ¹⁶In the same way, let your light shine before people, so they can see the good things you do and praise your Father who is in heaven.

Key Verse: "In the same way, let your light shine before people, so they can see the good things you do and praise your Father who is in heaven" (Matthew 5:16).

Connect

If you've ever had an occasion to visit a cavern or a mine, your tour guide might have taken you down to the lowest places and said, "Just to show everyone how very dark it is down here, I'm going to shut off the lights for just ten seconds. Stay where you are, and be prepared to experience complete darkness."

This happened to me when I visited a cavern in the mountains of North Carolina. Suffice it to say no dark room above ground can compare to the utter darkness of a cavern.

There is a primal comfort light brings. Perhaps it is part of our human makeup that goes back even before Bible times. Whether it's a campfire, a torch, or a lamp, a light in the darkness is a welcome sight. And in our modern world (at least before the days of GPS), one could experience comfort when driving down a dark rural road at night and finally seeing the lights of a motel vacancy sign.

In this lesson, Jesus speaks to the importance of his disciples being "the light of the world" (Matthew 5:14). In Jesus' day, a light at night was important for safety and security. And the collective lights of a city told travelers where to go to find shelter and hospitality.

Ironically, there have sometimes been occasions when light brought danger. For example,

116 Adult Bible Studies Teacher

if your class members are of the World War II generation (or during the early days of the Cold War), they might remember doing blackout drills. These were coordinated efforts to turn out all the lights and pull down all the shades in a community so as to make it harder for enemy bomber pilots to find a populated target.

I'm grateful that the only time household light has been a problem for my generation is on Halloween night when we run out of candy. We make every effort to turn out the household lights, from the front porch to the interior lamps, lest a child ring the doorbell, say "trick or treat," and we find we have nothing to give them.

When Jesus told his disciples that they were the light of the world, he was talking about a light far more significant than my household lights on Halloween or even city lights in wartime. He was speaking to his closest followers at the beginning of his public ministry (in Matthew's chronology) about their significance in God's kingdom-building work. As Gary Thompson says in our student book lesson, "The light that emanates from us is the reflected light of Jesus." This light has cosmic and eternal significance.

Jesus will also teach us this week that our light cannot and should not be hidden. Being the light of the world comes with evangelistic responsibilities. It is a gift to be able to show forth God's light in the world. A mature disciple of Jesus does not cover up this light. In fact, she does everything she can to let the light shine through her. Student book writer Gary Thompson put it this way: "Our mission is [to] shine God's light in the darkness, to share divine love, and to serve others in his name."

As you teach this lesson, remember that you are the light of the world. As the Holy Spirit illuminates the text for you, as you then share that light with your class members, and as they walk in the light of God in their lives, you are together being the "a city on top of a hill [that] can't be hidden" (Matthew 5:14).

Inspect

Let's get some context. At the end of Matthew 4, we read, "Jesus traveled throughout Galilee" and that "news about him spread throughout Syria" (Matthew 4:23, 24). As he was traveling and healing diseases, "large crowds followed him from Galilee, the Decapolis, Jerusalem, Judea, and from the areas beyond the Jordan River" (4:25).

But when Chapter 5 begins, we can't be sure just where Jesus was. All we know is that "he went up a mountain" (Matthew 5:1). That's why Matthew 5–7 was given the title "Sermon on the Mount." Some believe that Jesus was on a hill known as Mount Eremos in northern Israel.

Who else was with Jesus? Matthew says that when Jesus saw the crowds, he went up a mountain himself, and "his disciples came to him" (verse 1). But by the conclusion of the sermon, a crowd was listening that was "amazed at his teaching" (7:28) and subsequently followed him "when he had come down from the mountain" (8:1). Throughout the sermon, Jesus seems to be talking variously to two groups: his disciples and a larger public.

The text for this lesson is about how Jesus' disciples are "the light of the world" (5:14). This is only one metaphor among many that Jesus employed in the sermon. He most closely paired this light metaphor with a metaphor about salt (verse 13).

The Sermon on the Mount has long been regarded as an essential expression of Jesus' ethical teaching. Much of the same teaching is found in Luke 6:17-49 (known as the Sermon on the Plain), though not including this week's teaching on light.

Matthew 5:1-2. Jesus went up the mountain when he saw the crowds. It's not clear here whether he expected them to follow him.

Jesus' mountain ascent probably reminded Matthew's early readers of Moses' ascent of Mount Sinai. Elsewhere in Matthew, mountains are the setting of prayer (Matthew 14:23), healing (15:29), revelation (17:1; 28:16), and teaching (24:3).

Today, we would expect someone who is teaching a crowd to stand up. But in Jesus' time, it was customary for the synagogue teacher to sit to deliver the sermon.

Most of our English translations do not capture the full significance of Matthew 5:2 when they write, "He taught them." The Greek literally says, "He opened his mouth." With the opening of his mouth, the Son of God delivered his great sermon!

Verse 13. Since the salt and light metaphors seem to come as a pair, let's take a look at the salt metaphor.

Jesus said that his disciples and followers are the salt of the earth. Why did he tie together salt and earth? Was he referring to fertilizer? Wouldn't an overabundance of salt make for poor soil quality? It is possible to read too much into the connection between salt and earth.

But what exactly is "salt" in a disciple? Does it refer to a disciple's wisdom, winsomeness, charisma, or power of proclamation? Jesus left the metaphor open to some interpretation.

There is little to no doubt among scholars, however, that Jesus was using salt as a metaphor because of its usefulness as a food additive and/or preservative. There is something salty about a Jesus-follower.

Jesus thought of salt as something a disciple could somehow lose. We are left to wonder how salt could lose saltiness. Theories abound. But Jesus was apparently not concerned with how. He was more concerned with the fate of a salt-free disciple. Such a person will be rendered useless and subject to judgment. An unsalty disciple is compared to the dirt upon which we walk!

Luke's version of Jesus' salt metaphor says that unsalted disciples are of no value, "neither for the soil nor for the manure pile," but includes no judgment prediction (Luke 14:34-35).

Mark's version (Mark 9:50) is similar to Matthew's but adds a directive to the disciples: "Maintain salt among yourselves and keep peace with each other."

Jesus expressed a positive and then a negative side to the salt metaphor: "You are the salt of the earth," he said. "But if salt loses its saltiness. . . ." (Matthew 5:13). He drew the same positive/negative dichotomy with the light metaphor: "You are the light of the world," but people do not place the lamp under a basket (verse 15).

Verse 14. "You are the light of the world," Jesus told the disciples. Keep in mind that Jesus' disciples and most of his early followers were not noble, wealthy, or famous people. Many were laborers from the working or merchant classes. And as Jews living in the experiential darkness of a Roman-dominated province, they were probably not accustomed to being called "light."

Light in the Hebrew Bible was something God created and separated into night and day. When Jesus told them that they were "the light *of the world*" (italics added), he was making a theological claim. He was saying that his followers are significant in God's cosmic plan of redemption.

The biblical passages in which light is associated with good and darkness with evil are too numerous to list here. But look back to Matthew 4:16 to see how Jesus already used the light metaphor from Isaiah 9:2. "*The people who lived in the dark have seen a great light, and a light has come upon those who lived in the region and in shadow of death.*" In that verse, the light symbolized the new hope Jesus brought through the coming of God's reign.

Even though Jesus did not elaborate on why he chose the light metaphor, the significance was clear. In God's kingdom, it doesn't matter if you are wealthy, powerful, or famous. A follower of Jesus is as essential and significant as the light of God's creation!

Interestingly, in John's Gospel, Jesus says that he himself is the "light of the world" (John 8:12). And in Philippians 2:15, Paul says though his readers are surrounded by people "who are crooked and corrupt," they "shine like the stars in the world."

"A city on top of a hill can't be hidden." In Jesus' time, people could find the cities at night by their collective lights. The same thing happens today when we drive along a dark rural road at night until we begin to see the lights of inns, convenience stores, and restaurants.

This city is a metaphor for Jesus' disciples who, with their collective lights, resemble a city. And just as one doesn't put a cover over the light of a whole city, one doesn't put their lamp light under a basket (Matthew 5:15). The city's location on the top of a hill also makes it impossible to hide.

The new light of the world was also politically significant. That the world even needs the light of Jesus' disciples implies that the world is in darkness. God's people have often been described as lights unto the nations (for example, Isaiah 42:6; 49:6).

Though Jesus is the light (John 8:12), his light shines in the world through his disciples and followers. Just like salt, the disciples' light is indispensable. Their very presence in the world dispels the darkness. And like a city on the hill, their light will be visible from a distance.

We should not go so far as to assume that Jesus was talking here about the city of God, the New Jerusalem from Revelation. Jesus spoke of the city in this way in his more apocalyptic statements elsewhere in the Gospels.

Verse 15. Most of us have become accustomed to having instant light at our fingertips. If we cannot reach the light switch on the wall, we need only use the flashlight on our cell phones. With the invention of LED light bulbs, long-lasting, low-power light has become universal.

In Jesus' time, however, people had to gather their own lamp oil, trim their own wick, and put out their own light at night. Many people in the developing world still must do this today. Once they went to the trouble of lighting a lamp, they would not cover it. If they needed to darken the room, they would probably just put the lamp outside the room.

Jesus implied an economy of the lamp and its light. A light and its oil should not be wasted. To put a basket or bowl over the lamp would be ridiculous. The measuring vessel Jesus mentioned held about one peck (or 8.75 liters) of grain.

When a lamp was lit in a household, it was hung from a stand so as to provide maximum illumination. Not only should a lamp not be covered, it should be raised up for the benefit of all.

This is a parallel point to the one Jesus made in verse 14 about how the light of a city on a hill cannot be hidden. If Jesus' disciples are the "light of the world," they should not be hidden in a household or on a hill. Jesus made this abundantly clear in verse 16.

Verse 16. Here we have Jesus' own explanation of his light metaphor. Lest his point be lost on his listeners, he explained that each disciple should "let [their] light shine before people." Jesus exhorted them to let their light shine and accomplish its purpose.

In one sense, the very fact that they were his disciples made them "the light of the world" (verse 14), but Jesus quickly linked their discipleship light to action. They should let their light shine "before people" (verse 16).

Their light was not just for their own edification and illumination in a world of darkness. Other people should benefit from their light. Perhaps they would be drawn to the light as a traveler may be on a lonely stretch of road at night. And perhaps people will desire the light of Christian discipleship for themselves.

These may all be true, but Jesus' stated reason for letting their light shine "before people" is so that "they can see the good things you do" (verse 16). And by seeing these "good things you do," other people may "praise your Father who is in heaven" (verse 16).

Being the light of the world is wonderful! Shining that light into the darkness is even more wonderful. Letting that light shine so people see it is still even more wonderful. And the best of all is that when they see the light, they will praise God! The true end for which all the light-shining is going on is to bring praise to God.

At the end of the day, our light is not all about making individual Christians look good. It's not all about attracting people to our institutional churches. It's not even about shining a spotlight on Jesus who himself is the Light of the World (John 8:12). The whole point of being Jesus' light-filled disciples is to glorify God.

Mark 9:49-50. We will look at two passages that roughly parallel the Matthew text: Mark 9:49-50 and Luke 14:34-35.

Mark does not have a saying about light per se. But in Mark 9:49, Jesus makes a brief reference to salt, saying, "Everyone will be salted with fire." This phrase seems enigmatic until you read what comes right before it: a judgment statement.

In the previous judgment statement (verses 47-48), Jesus warned against causing "the little ones who believe in me to trip up and fall into sin" (verse 42). One who does so will "be thrown into hell" (verse 47).

We've probably all heard or used the phrase "pouring salt on a wound." That's what Jesus means here in verse 49: The fire of judgment will be compounded by the pain of salt.

But Mark 9:50 uses salt in an entirely different way. Rather than salt as a punishment, Jesus says, "Salt is good." He goes on to state something similar to Matthew 5:13 about salt losing its saltiness.

Mark is considered by most scholars to be the oldest of the Gospels in our Bible. The phrase "If salt loses its saltiness, how will it become salty again" (Mark 9:50) could have been one of Matthew's sources for this lesson's text.

Finally, in Mark's account, Jesus adds an admonishment to his disciples to "maintain salt among [themselves] and keep peace with each other" (verse 50). Their saltiness would keep them focused on the unity of their shared ministry. Similarly, in Colossians 4:6, Paul advises, "Let your speech always be gracious, seasoned with salt, so that you may know how you ought to answer everyone" (NRSV) who challenges your faith.

Luke 11:33. Like Mark, Luke has his own parallel to the salt metaphor in Luke 14:34-35. It is virtually identical to the Focal Passage for this lesson. So we will focus on Luke's brief light metaphor in Luke 11:33.

The context is that a crowd had grown around Jesus just as he began to pronounce a judgment on "this generation" (Luke 11:29).

In verse 33, Luke includes Jesus' teaching that "people don't light a lamp and then put it in a closet or under a basket. Rather, they place the lamp on a lampstand so that those who enter the house can see the light." Already, you can probably see the similarities to Matthew 5:15.

Reflect

How might you creatively teach this passage on light this Sunday? Not every Bible text is so relatable and so visceral as one on light. Add to that the companion metaphor of salt just before our Focal Passage, and this could be a multisensory lesson!

Keep in mind what educators say about how people learn differently. In Christian education, we have so often limited ourselves to one teaching/learning style: the lecture. This was the dominant style in schools through the middle of the twentieth century. Is that the style of teaching in your class?

Through the latter half of the twentieth century and into today, some Sunday school classes and other groups have adopted a seminar style.

The seminar might start with a lecture by the teacher and then evolve into a discussion among the students. Hence resources like this one include discussion questions meant to complement the seminar style.

Today, there is growing awareness of multisensory learning styles. Educators refer to visual, auditory, kinesthetic, and tactile learners (or seeing, hearing, doing, and touching). In the case of teaching a lesson that involves salt and light, we should think about how to teach through taste and seeing.

As you can see in "Inspect," I've taken the liberty of pointing out that our text on light is paired with Jesus' teaching on salt. Think about how you could use that in your teaching (without entirely distracting the class from the lesson on light).

Perhaps class members will enjoy talking about how they use salt. Some put salt on everything. Others may have been relegated to a low-salt or salt-free diet. To use the sense of taste, you might put a salt-free cracker and a saltine at each class member's seat. They could try a bite of each and compare the difference. I'm no food scientist, but I'm given to understand that the salt on a salted cracker stimulates our salivary glands and makes it easier for us to eat the absorbent cracker.

When it comes to light, you have a variety of options. What can you do to the meeting space before class members come in? Will you leave the overhead lights off? put dark shades over the windows? hold the class this week in a windowless room in the church building and turn out the lights?

Another possibility could involve a lamp. I have a nineteenth-century antique oil lamp that my grandmother left me. I haven't lit it in a couple of decades. A friend who has been to the Holy Land brought me back a traditional oil lamp from the region. Maybe you or someone in your class has such an item. Even a modern camping lantern or flashlight would suffice.

If you have the *Adult Bible Studies* DVD, review it ahead of time, and determine when in the course of your discussion you will show it to your class.

Start the class discussion with a superficial introduction to the light metaphor. Say: ***In today's text, Jesus tells the disciples that they are the "light of the world" (Matthew 5:14).*** Then ask: ***What does that metaphor mean to you? What do you think Jesus meant by it?***

The discussion is bound to go in many different directions as students roll the metaphor around in their imaginations. Some may readily identify with being the light of the world. They may point to how others can know Jesus' light and love through them.

Others may be reluctant to imagine themselves as the "light of the world" (Matthew 5:14). In their humility, they may be cautious about such a bold statement. After all, some could recall Jesus' own statement in John that he is the light of the world (John 8:12).

It may help to remind your more reticent students that Jesus was talking to his disciples at the start of the Sermon on the Mount. Though we may be overwhelmed by the responsibility of being Jesus' light in the world, Jesus obviously wanted his disciples to embrace this role.

It will help to explore with the class why Jesus wanted his disciples to think of themselves as the light of the world. Say: *Jesus told his disciples that they were the light of the world because he wanted others to see the light in them. In Matthew 5:15-16, Jesus says that they are to be seen like a city on a hill or an uncovered lamp on a lampstand. "In the same way," he says, "let your light shine before people" (Matthew 5:16).*

Jesus didn't ask his disciples if they were all right with this. He just told them it was so. Likewise, he does not give us the option to cover our light with a basket or bowl. He does not let us opt out of being the light of the world. He implies that it would be foolish to cover our light.

Consider Gary Thompson's illustration at the beginning of the lesson in the student book in which a child looks at the saints in the stained glass windows at church and concludes that the saints are those who let the light in. Rightly so!

Jesus was not telling the disciples that they were so smart or strong or good that they were the true source of God's light in the world. He was also not saying, "Don't be so modest."

Stress that Jesus was saying that the light of the kingdom of God was seen in them. Ask: *But why do we resist this truth? What holds us back?*

We cannot forget the last verse in which Jesus tells us why our light should shine before people: "so they can see the good things you do and praise your Father who is in heaven" (Matthew 5:16).

The praise ultimately goes to God. The credit is not even supposed to be ours, if that's what's bothering us. Think about it. We didn't invent the light. God did. And this was important in ancient Hebrew theology. God spoke the light into being (Genesis 1:3) and separated the light from the darkness (verse 4). The light came from God and predated human beings.

You may find these reminders helpful if your class members are reticent to accept their calling to be the "light of the world." Let's be patient with ourselves and with them. We are like those disciples who followed Jesus up the mount and sat down and heard this sermon. It's natural that we may feel intimidated. But it also shows Jesus' great grace that he would include us in his work in the world.

Say: *Any great moral teacher could encourage his or her followers to do good works. But Jesus went much further. He said, "You are the light of the world" (Matthew 5:14). What does he want others to see through us?*

We don't do good works just to feel better about ourselves (that's altruism). We don't do good works so our church can seem busier and better than the church down the street.

We do these good works, Jesus says here, because that is who we are. They are an expression of the stature we already possess as the light of the world. We are salt. We are light.

And we do these good things, as Jesus said, so we can "praise [our] Father who is in heaven" (Matthew 5:16). What a wonderful way to praise God by accepting God's image of us as salt and light and to live into that!

Jesus warns us against doing anything less! Salt that has lost its saltiness is "good for nothing except to be thrown away" (Matthew 5:13). Light that is hidden under a basket is a waste of lamp oil and a fire hazard, too.

Say: *Consider what a disservice we do to Christ's name if we squander his faith in us. What does it say to the world if we are God's salt and light, but we keep that to ourselves? How must it make God feel if we rob the world of the good gift God has given through us?*

Close by praying together the prayer at the end of the lesson in the student book:

Dear God, we pray today for the gifts of wisdom and vision to discern your will and hear your call, for the gift of faith to overcome our doubts, and for the gift of courage to keep us single-minded in our commitment to your cause so that we will faithfully carry out whatever mission you give us. Fill our hearts with the love and compassion that will motivate us to shed your light; in Jesus' name we pray. Amen.

February 20 | Lesson 12
Informing, Transforming Faith

Focal Passage
James 1:19-27

Background Text
Same

Purpose
To better understand the relationship between belief and practice

James 1:19-27
¹⁹Know this, my dear brothers and sisters: everyone should be quick to listen, slow to speak, and slow to grow angry. ²⁰This is because an angry person doesn't produce God's righteousness. ²¹Therefore, with humility, set aside all moral filth and the growth of wickedness, and welcome the word planted deep inside you—the very word that is able to save you.

²²You must be doers of the word and not only hearers who mislead themselves. ²³Those who hear but don't do the word are like those who look at their faces in a mirror. ²⁴They look at themselves, walk away, and immediately forget what they were like. ²⁵But there are those who study the perfect law, the law of freedom, and continue to do it. They don't listen and then forget, but they put it into practice in their lives. They will be blessed in whatever they do.

²⁶If those who claim devotion to God don't control what they say, they mislead themselves. Their devotion is worthless. ²⁷True devotion, the kind that is pure and faultless before God the Father, is this: to care for orphans and widows in their difficulties and to keep the world from contaminating us.

Key Verse: "You must be doers of the word and not only hearers who mislead themselves" (James 1:22).

Connect

Throughout this unit, we are looking at how we participate in God's work through our actions. It turns out that it matters what we do, not just what we believe. When God honors us with the gift of faith, there are certain responsibilities attached. Just as we read in the previous lesson, we should never squander the trust and responsibility God has invested in us.

This applies to how we interact with other believers and with critics. When James wrote this epistle, he was instructing his readers on how to behave as Christ-followers. The whole book of James is full of practical instruction. Do this. Don't do that.

But James is not a book of simple moralisms. There is a coherent point to all these admonitions and instructions. By combining their faith with their actions, Christians practice "true devotion" (James 1:27).

In the nine verses we will consider in this lesson, we will encounter three emphases: (1) being quick to listen and slow to speak (verses 19-21); (2) being doers of the word and not hearers only (verses 22-25); and (3) the nature of true devotion (verses 26-27).

As you prepare to teach this lesson, consider how James's admonitions apply to your own life. Do you find yourself being quick to speak and slow to listen? Can you relate to the challenge of adding action to your beliefs? Where do you see evidence of "true devotion" (verse 27) in your life and in the lives of other Christians you admire?

Such faithfulness requires an ability to look inward. As we will see in "Inspect" regarding verse 23, James tells us to turn our critical gaze inward as if we are looking in a mirror. We should radically reform our own lives based on what Jesus has taught us.

The test of our true devotion will come in how we treat the most vulnerable among us. James speaks specifically of "orphans and widows" (verse 27). Readers of James will find that he often returned to the theme of justice for the less fortunate. Like Jesus, James believed that "one's life does not consist in the abundance of possessions" (Luke 12:15, NRSV).

A Bible study session on James is always sure to bring lively discussion. His epistle is seen as one of the Bible's most accessible books for the modern reader. Be prepared to field lots of intriguing examples and comparisons from your class members as they apply these verses to their own lives.

All the while, keep in mind that the overarching purpose for studying this passage is "to better understand the relationship between belief and practice." James puts his readers (including us) on trial. He makes us look in the mirror and make sure that we are walking the walk, not just talking the talk.

Inspect

Tradition has posited that the writer of the Epistle (or Letter) of James is none other than James the brother of Jesus (also known as James the Just). It was long assumed that James, Jesus' brother, might have received a vision of Jesus after Jesus' earthly ministry, as the Gospel of John states that Jesus' brothers didn't believe in him (John 7:5).

Paul referred to Jesus' brother James as an "apostle" (Galatians 1:19). But Martin Luther famously cast doubt on the authorship of James and generally disregarded it. He called it an epistle of straw!

Modern scholarship has cast doubts on the traditional assumption that the author of James was Jesus' brother. Perhaps the letter was added to by Christians who later wrote under James's name.

In any event, we should not confuse this James with James the son of Zebedee and brother of John whom Jesus called as disciples in Matthew 4:21-22 and Mark 1:19-20. That apostle James (also known as James the Great) was killed by Herod Agrippa I in Acts 12:1-2.

Even more difficult than the authorship question is the dating question. If James the brother of Jesus wrote this, it would have been before 62 to 69 AD when he was martyred. However, James's mention of elders in the church would indicate that the book was written sometime later after the church had begun to organize.

James 1:19-27. The text for this lesson is a series of three general exhortations at the end of James's opening chapter. Many scholars contend that James contains a series of loosely connected wisdom reflections and moral appeals. The writer's intention was to teach the "twelve tribes who are scattered outside the land of Israel" (James 1:1) how (and how not) to put their newfound Christian faith into action.

It would appear that James 1:19-27 is a collection of three exhortations. The first is on speech behavior (verses 19-21). The second is on hearing and doing (verses 22-25). And the third is on pure religion (verses 26-27).

These three wisdom teachings are connected to important points James raised elsewhere. For example, in the rest of Chapter 1, James referenced tests, maturity, perfection, wisdom, wealth, blessedness, and temptation. We could make a case that James 1:19-27 is designed to sum up the rest of Chapter 1's points.

Verses 19-21. This is James's assault on the immorality and destructiveness of an uncontrolled tongue. Everyone should be quick to listen and slow to speak. Notice that he did not say how much listening or speaking he expected. Rather, he commented on how one should listen first and speak later.

Remember, James was writing to early Jewish Christians who had been going through difficult trials. What does someone want to do in distress? Speak up! Long and loud! But James believed a wise Christ-follower should do the opposite. One who is quick to listen and slow to speak may be better able to avoid sin. As he explained in James 3:1-12, the tongue is powerful and should be tamed.

If those who were fighting with James's readers were unbelievers, perhaps the humility and economy of words of the Christians would make a positive impression on bystanders. It would give the impression that Jesus's followers are people of peace who are confident in their beliefs. James had just written that conflicts are opportunities for testing that can develop maturity if handled properly.

Verse 20 is difficult to translate. English versions vary, but the intention behind the words is to contrast wrath with the life and justice God desires. The anger James had in mind is not the justifiable defensiveness the Christians felt for their faith community. It was a wrathful, hand-wringing desire to do damage to others that concerned James.

Such wrathful hatred does not produce justice. Think about our best ideals for our justice system, for example. The most just societies in the world do not let their courtrooms be ruled by wrath or vengeance but by truth-seeking and the fair treatment of all.

As Jesus said, "Everyone who is angry with their brother or sister will be in danger of judgment" (Matthew 5:22). Jesus was not referring to a righteous anger that reacts to injustice. He was referring to a writhing ill-will that damages human relationships. Such malice "doesn't produce God's righteousness" (James 1:20).

"Therefore," James added in verse 21, "with humility, set aside all moral filth and the growth of wickedness." He would have us remember that he was not just giving us a list of do's and don'ts. He was describing an ethic of personal behavior marked by humility. And he believed that this morality is incompatible with wickedness.

Accepting the way of Christ necessitates the rejection of evil. When people in our Methodist tradition come for baptism, confirmation, or church membership, I ask them if they profess Jesus as Lord. But I also ask them, "Do you renounce the spiritual forces of wickedness, reject the evil powers of this world, and repent of your sin?" Furthermore, I ask, "Do you accept the freedom and power God gives you to resist evil, injustice, and oppression in whatever forms they present themselves?" In this way, we show that following Jesus necessitates a rejection of wickedness.

In verse 21, James returned to verse 19 to restate his commands. Those who have "set aside all moral filth and the growth of wickedness" should promote a different kind of growth: the growth of "the word planted deep inside." Rather than wrath and wickedness, the Christian should nourish justice, peace, and love, especially in her speech.

Readers of Ephesians might find a parallel in Ephesians 4:22, 25, where Christians are urged to put off the old self and its falsehood. Those who read the epistles of Peter will also see there an emphasis on getting rid of all evil that we might crave the word of God (1 Peter 2:1-2).

Verses 22-25. From his exhortation on spiritually proper speech, James moved right along to his exhortation on hearing and doing. The old King James Version was often quoted to me as a child: "Be ye doers of the word, and not hearers only."

I did not realize how this verse is so connected to what came before. The focus has moved from the implanted word (verse 21) to the lived-out word (verse 22). Just as we are to welcome "the word planted deep inside" (verse 21), we are to re-express that word through our actions. People who fail to do this don't just fall down on the job, they "mislead themselves" (verse 22). There is something corrupt about hearing but not doing.

We may recognize echoes of God's claim that God's word "comes from my mouth; it does not return to me empty. Instead, it does what I want, and accomplishes what I intend" (Isaiah 55:11). This is also consistent with James's later emphasis on the connection between faith and works (James 2:14-26). The amazing thing is that God catches up the hearers of the word like us and makes us doers, too!

When we are hearers and doers, we are persevering in the moral formation James referred to in 1:1-18. We are moving away from hypocrisy and toward humility.

In verses 23 and 24, we learn the follies of those "who hear but don't do" (verse 23). They are like those who "look at their faces in a mirror" (verse 23). But then they "walk away, and immediately forget what they were like" (verse 24).

This is a parable in which the person does not have the power of self-evaluation. James was not necessarily suggesting that they are narcissistic in the way Narcissus could not pull himself away from his own reflection.

The power of the comparison is in the person's forgetfulness. Their act of looking is incomplete when they look away and forget. It does not give them the insight James would want them to have.

The Greek literally means "they forget their own existence or birth." James's Jewish-Christian audience knew that all people are created in the image of God. So to forget one's birth/existence is to forget one's divine image-bearing.

In contrast, James hoped his readers would look into the mirror, which is to "study the perfect law, the law of freedom, and continue to do it" (verse 25). Here, he filled out the parable by telling us more about the mirror. The mirror is one of knowledge, not just of self-evaluation or perfect sight (as in Paul's use of the term in 1 Corinthians 13:12). It is not made of mixtures of silver and tin but of the "perfect law" by which James probably meant Torah.

The Greek philosopher Plutarch once remarked that when students listen to lectures, they should examine themselves in light of what they learned. He said a student who did not apply to himself what he had learned was like a man who got up from a barber's chair, touched his head to make sure the haircut had been done, and then left without looking in a mirror.

James's "dear brothers and sisters" (verse 19) should "put [the law] into practice in their lives" (verse 25). They are given a promise (not unlike a beatitude): "They will be blessed in whatever they do" (verse 25). Just like in verse 12, this blessing pertains to God's favor on a person. It is also applied to "whatever they do"; in other words, their doing as doers of the word. They will be blessed not *because* of the doing, but *in* the doing.

Verses 26-27. The third and final of James's exhortations at the end of Chapter 1 is about pure religion. He offered examples of the active obedience of one who is a hearer and doer of the word. Again, he contrasted two kinds of religion: religion as an adjective (verse 26) and religion as a noun (verse 27).

James set forth that even among those who practiced the outward manifestations of religion, there were some who practiced a deceptive religion. Note that he was not condemning all people who practiced outward manifestations of religion. Some were pure and faultless in their practices. This text should not be misread as a pejorative against formalism. James's concern was with religion that is worthy of the name, instead of "worthless" (verse 26).

The first example is a negative one: those who "don't control what they say" (verse 26). As in James 1:19 and in James 3:1-12, he was concerned with the use of language and the tongue. He put the control of the tongue ahead of the outward signs of religiosity. In so doing, James was actually consistent with the Torah itself that repeatedly emphasizes the care of right speech.

Two things happen to those who do not "bridle their tongues" (verse 26, NRSV): (1) they deceive their hearts, and (2) their religion is worthless. They jeopardize their relationship with others and their blessedness before God.

The second example of right religion is a positive one: "to care for orphans and widows in their difficulties and to keep the world from contaminating us" (verse 27). This is the fruit of "true devotion, the kind that is pure and faultless before God" (verse 27).

James was well-known for his Torah piety (Acts 15:16-18), but even he did not center all of Jewish purity around the Temple practices. He saw purity as an internal condition that transcends externalities. For James, to be "pure and faultless before God" (verse 27) meant to be marked off from those who are unjust, oppressive, and worldly. It was devotion to the Torah as well as the compassion called for therein. This is true devotion.

Rather than writing in vague generalities, James got specific. This pure and undefiled religion can be recognized in the "care for orphans and widows in their difficulties" (verse 27).

Dual concern for orphans and widows goes back to passages like Ezekiel 22:7 and Isaiah 1:17. Ancient papyri have shown that being an orphan happened when one lost at least one parent, not necessarily both. Widows, too, were of special concern because they might not be brought into the household of a male relative, often their only viable source of provisions after the death of their husbands.

Our United Methodist tradition is like many in the world in that we have established orphanages, foster homes, and senior-living establishments. There, we give special attention to the vulnerable, young and old.

Finally, an indicator of pure and undefiled religion is "to keep the world from contaminating us" (verse 27). Some translations say "unstained." We should not be surprised by this. James spent most of Chapter 1 warning his brothers and sisters against those who posed a threat to them, especially from within the faith community.

Also, we know that James's view of the world was a negative one, influenced by the dualism in Greek thought of his time. He was not referring to the world in the same sense as Genesis 1, which God called "good." He warned (especially in 3:15) against that which is worldly or earthly, that is, human forceful efforts to establish order that are at odds with God's will.

Reflect

As I said in "Connect," a study of the Book of James is sure to bring lively discussion. He wrote in an accessible way using a lot of what we today call "common sense" wisdom. There are just so many relatable verses in James's writing that, in some ways, it will be easy for your class to get away from the main purpose of our lesson.

To ensure that you do not lose sight of it, write the lesson's Purpose Statement on the classroom board or flipchart. If you have the *Adult Bible Studies* DVD, begin by showing the segment related to this lesson.

Then give the class context about the Epistle of James before getting into the Focal Passage. The material at the beginning of "Inspect" may help. You can also consult a reliable Bible commentary or ask your pastor. In this way, you might help the class not rush too quickly to the application of this text before they begin to understand what it meant to James's first readers.

Explain that you will be reading from the Book of James, a popular and accessible book of the New Testament. You will be reading three admonitions James gave to new Jewish Christians about how to deal with one another and with their detractors.

Say: ***Think about a time when you felt you had to defend your beliefs. What was the most difficult part of that?***

Examples might include a conversation about religion with an atheist or a skeptic. Perhaps someone in your class has children or grandchildren who have drifted away from the faith of their childhood. Ask: ***Do you feel you can talk about your faith with that family member?***

Explain that James's original audience was facing the same challenges, some of which were coming from their Jewish friends and family who did not believe that Jesus was the Messiah. Now read aloud James's first exhortation in James 1:19-21 about being "quick to listen, slow to speak, and slow to grow angry."

Ask: ***How does it make you feel when your beliefs are challenged? Do you want to lash out? Do you want to yell and shout? Do you grow angry quickly? James cautions against such reactions. Why do you suppose he did that?***

Note, it appears that James wanted to protect the dignity of others in public and private discourse. He believed that nothing good comes from an argument. Ultimately, it can even make understanding more difficult and alienate people who might otherwise come to believe in Jesus as the Messiah.

James was talking about the importance of taming the tongue. Class members will likely be familiar with his longer statement on the power of the tongue in James 3:1-12. As time permits, read aloud this relevant passage.

Say: ***Along with his concern for proper speech and behavior, James was concerned about whether we are "doers of the word" or "only hearers" (James 1:22). You have probably heard that phrase before. What does it mean to you to be a doer and not just a hearer?***

Ask class members to consider the importance of pairing action with belief. Someone may quote James 2:17: "In the same way, faith is dead when it doesn't result in faithful activity." That is a good parallel to James 1:22.

Consider the opening illustration in the lesson in the student book. It tells us about a pastor who asked his students what they do when they come across a command in Scripture. He hoped someone would say, "I try to follow the command." But instead, one student replied, "I underline them in blue."

Suggest that at least she was paying attention to the commands in Scripture. But that would not be enough for James. The Law, the Torah, and the teachings of Jesus must be put into practice and action.

At this point, consider taking the discussion in an interesting direction by explaining the meaning of verses 23 and 24 and the mirror metaphor. Information from "Inspect" may prove useful in doing so. Point out what James meant by looking in a mirror: true self-examination.

Stress that James said we should look at ourselves in a mirror but not walk away immediately, forgetting what we look like. Rather, we should examine ourselves. We should look within.

Ask: **What do you see when you look within at your discipleship? Do you like what you see?**

These are challenging questions. Class members may not be ready to answer them out loud. Give them time to reflect. Remember, as the teacher, you will often feel that time is passing slowly when you are not talking. Be patient. Eventually, someone may dare to be first to speak.

In addition, do your own reflection on this question before your class meets. Wait as long as you can for someone else to answer first. But be prepared to give your own testimony, too. Perhaps your honesty will help them feel more comfortable. When did you look within yourself and find your discipleship lacking? How did that make you feel? Did you do anything in response to your realizations or did you just walk away from the mirror?

Stress that James does not want us to look within ourselves and then walk away from the mirror, forgetting what we've seen. He would have us put our faith into action. Specifically, he wants his readers to practice what he calls "true devotion" (James 1:27).

By that he means controlling what we say (1:19, 26), being doers of the word and not hearers only, and by caring for the most vulnerable.

Reread James 1:27 to the class, and ask: **What does James say here that is so important?** (*Hopefully, someone will point to the emphasis on orphans and widows.*)

Summarize what is in "Inspect" about how and why orphans and widows were particularly vulnerable people in the Bible's time and place. These are important populations. Challenge the class to come up with other vulnerable groups today. Write them on the board as they brainstorm. For example, someone might mention the sick, immigrants, addicts, or others.

With a comprehensive list of vulnerable populations in front of them, encourage the class members to take it all in. Look at the list with them, and reflect on the enormity of need in the world.

Say: **Our purpose today is "to better understand the relationship between belief and practice."** Ask: **What do we need to do for these vulnerable groups if we are to put our faith into practice?**

Write their ideas on the board. Some will mention outreach and mission efforts your church are already part of. Others may come up with new ideas that need to be considered. In some cases, a church group might be at a loss to describe how they are addressing the needs of vulnerable populations.

Remember, this is your class looking in the mirror as James told them to do. Don't let them look in and then casually walk away (as James warned against in verses 23-24). Stay with the awkwardness of the question. Then ask the class to identify at least one vulnerable population with which they do not currently engage as people of faith. Find at least one area in which they have been hearers but not doers.

Challenge your class to address that shortcoming. Put it on the agenda for next week's class. You don't necessarily need to bring this before your entire congregation. You don't even have to have all the answers for how to help everyone. The important thing is "to better understand the relationship between belief and practice" and then to do more than just understand it, but to respond with action. Lead class members to consider what they can do as individuals, and what you might do together as a class, to address at least one of these needs among vulnerable populations.

To close, pray together the prayer at the end of the lesson in the student book: **Dear God, we know that your love never fails, your blessings never cease, and your grace is always sufficient. Help us to recognize that knowing your word is useless unless we put it into practice; in Jesus' name we pray. Amen.**

February 27 | Lesson 13
The Great Commission

Focal Passages
Matthew 28:16-20

Background Text
Same

Purpose
To explore what it means to make disciples

Matthew 28:16-20
16 Now the eleven disciples went to Galilee, to the mountain where Jesus told them to go. 17 When they saw him, they worshipped him, but some doubted. 18 Jesus came near and spoke to them, "I've received all authority in heaven and on earth. 19 Therefore, go and make disciples of all nations, baptizing them in the name of the Father and of the Son and of the Holy Spirit, 20 teaching them to obey everything that I've commanded you. Look, I myself will be with you every day until the end of this present age."

Key Verse: "Therefore, go and make disciples of all nations, baptizing them in the name of the Father and of the Son and of the Holy Spirit" (Matthew 28:19).

Connect

I'm officially old enough that a movie I watched as a youth can now be called a classic. I have in mind the 1991 film *City Slickers*, starring Billy Crystal and Jack Palance. The ever-chilling Palance plays Curly, a grizzled old cowpoke who tells Crystal that the secret of life is "one thing. Just one thing."

"What is the 'one thing'?" Crystal asks.

"That's what *you* have to find out," comes the reply.[1]

People come to the Bible looking for the "one thing." The Bible is jam-packed with many passages we can apply to life. But what is the one passage that says it all? What one thing from the Bible is the most important?

The Greatest Commandments (Lesson 10) would be the one thing for many people who are looking for a rule for living. The Sermon on the Mount (Lesson 11) contains many other central tenets from Jesus' teachings.

But there is one passage that tells us what the one thing is when it comes to our mission as followers of Jesus. It is Jesus' ultimate instruction to his disciples for all time. All of these other imperatives are second to this "one thing."

We call it "the Great Commission."

Some of the most familiar passages of the Bible are given their own titles in the original Hebrew and Greek. For example, the *Shema* (Lesson 10) is named for its first word in Hebrew ("hear"). We also learned that the Greatest Commandment is referred to as such by Jesus in Matthew 22:38 and Mark 12:29. And the Ten Commandments ("ten words") are given their title in Exodus 34:28 and Deuteronomy 10:4.

But other well-known passages receive their titles not in the Hebrew or the Greek, but by church tradition. This is the case with the text for this lesson: "The Great Commission." Though neither Jesus nor Matthew used the words *great commission*, that is what we call it. And it is called "great" because of its primacy over the other commissions Jesus gave his disciples.

Jesus did give his 12 disciples other commissions. Jesus "gave them authority over unclean spirits to throw them out and to heal every disease and every sickness" (Matthew 10:1) before sending his 12 out "to the lost sheep, the people of Israel" (10:6). Jesus gave the Twelve similar commissions in Mark 6:7-13 and Luke 9:1-6.

And there were other instances after Jesus' resurrection when he gave his followers directives: Mark 16:15-18, Luke 24:47-49 (and its parallel in Acts 1:8), and John 20:21-23. These were mostly preaching commissions.

However, our text for this lesson is Jesus' most direct commission after his resurrection. It's the commission that he intended them (and us) to follow above all others. It is not limited to preaching. Jesus instructed his followers to teach and to baptize, thereby making disciples for him.

As you engage this text with your class, look for clues about what it means to make disciples of Jesus Christ. I've never found a Christian who outright rejected that commission. But I've found plenty of Christians who feel unsure about what that looks like and inadequate to the task. Let's break down the passage into understandable portions and see what Jesus meant.

Inspect

Before we look at our passage verse by verse, take a brief look at the whole chapter. Unlike Luke 24 and John 20–21, the distance from the empty tomb to the close of Matthew's Gospel is short. Jesus made one post-resurrection appearance to Mary Magdalene and another Mary (Matthew 28:9) in Matthew's Gospel before the 11 remaining disciples saw him and worshiped him (verse 17).

And how does the chapter end? Matthew chose to end his Gospel with Jesus' Great Commission. The last words of the whole first Gospel belong to Jesus alone. It is the exclamation point at the end of the whole book!

Our text for this lesson can be divided into two parts: (1) Jesus' resurrection appearance in verses 16-17 and (2) the Great Commission in verses 18-20.

Matthew 28:16. The subject of the story in verse 16 are the 11 remaining disciples who saw the risen Jesus. We know that Judas was no longer present because of his death (Matthew 27:3-10).

Mary Magdalene and the other Mary (28:1) encountered the risen Jesus first (verse 9). In that encounter, Jesus told the women, "Go and tell my brothers that I am going into Galilee. They will see me there" (verse 10). When we get to verse 16, we can presume that the two Marys had delivered their message to the 11 because "the eleven disciples went to Galilee, to the mountain where Jesus told them to go."

Galilee was an important location for them to meet. Jesus' ministry began in "Galilee of the Gentiles" (Matthew 4:15; Isaiah 9:1). It was where his community of disciples first became the church (Matthew 16:13, 18; Caesarea Philippi is located north of the Sea of Galilee).

Recall that Jesus told his disciples in Matthew 26:32, "After I'm raised up, I'll go before you to Galilee." Also, the angel at the tomb said to tell the disciples, "He's going on ahead of you to Galilee. You will see him there" (28:7).

The setting for this Resurrection appearance and Great Commission was also "the mountain" (verse 16). Significant events in Jesus' life took place on mountains: the temptation, the Sermon on the Mount (Lesson 11), and the Transfiguration (Lesson 7), for example. But just as we have been uncertain about the exact geographical location of these other mountains, we are not sure to what mountain Matthew is referring in verse 16. We are told that it was "the mountain where Jesus told them to go," but Matthew didn't include that earlier conversation in his Gospel.

Verse 17. In this particular Resurrection appearance, Jesus did not so much appear to the disciples as the disciples saw him. This time the disciples instantly recognized Jesus.

We were told in verse 9 that he appeared in a physical body such that the women could grab his feet and worship him. It's safe to assume this was the same physical form in which he appeared to the disciples in verse 17.

It is possible that the disciples also fell at his feet the way the women did in verse 9. Matthew says they worshiped him, which in the Greek has the connotation of falling prostrate on the floor before him, as was customary before a ruler.

However, readers are not prepared for the last words of this verse: "but some doubted." Scholars have debated what this meant. The commentaries of the ancient church seemed to apologize for the disciples when they theorized that there were other followers of Jesus in attendance who doubted while his 11 still believed. Other ancient writers wondered if the word for "doubted" referred to their past doubt only. But these interpretations have not held up to modern scrutiny.

Today's translators and scholars believe that Matthew was saying (1) the disciples each felt a mixture of worship and doubt, or (2) most disciples worshiped while a few of them still doubted. Most twentieth-century Bible translators have opted for the latter: "They worshipped him, but some doubted" (verse 17).

Here, Matthew did not use any of the usual Greek words for "disbelief." Instead, he used a more nuanced word that we find in only one other place: Matthew 14:31. On that occasion, Peter walked on the water; became afraid; and Jesus asked, "Why did you doubt?" It is the kind of doubt that amounts to hesitation or indecision. And just as they worshiped him in this text, ultimately Peter and the disciples worshiped Jesus in the boat despite this doubt (14:33).

We can sympathize with disciples who had mixed feelings when we consider all the disciples had just been through: the trauma of watching their Lord be crucified, dead, and buried. Now he was miraculously appearing before them.

They probably did not cognitively doubt it was Jesus whom they saw. They did not say, for example, "It's a ghost" (14:26)! Rather, Matthew is telling us that they were still in a state of uncertainty about what these recent events meant and what might happen next. And Matthew did not feel the need to explain their feelings or resolve them. He moved on to focus on Jesus' next actions and words.

Verse 18. The disciples saw Jesus in the last verse, but now "Jesus came near" them. This was meant to comfort them and perhaps assuage their doubts. He did not rebuke any of them for doubting, abandoning him in his trial and crucifixion, or denying him (Peter).

We're reminded of Jesus' emotional and spiritual intimacy with his apostles. We might think of the moment after Jesus' transfiguration, for example, when he "came and touched" Peter, James, and John as he told them not to be afraid (17:7).

Along with coming to them, Jesus "spoke to them," another act that must have comforted them (28:18). These are the first words the 11 disciples heard from their Savior after his resurrection. There was no initial question from the disciples. They made no reply. Jesus' words made it clear that he had moved on from the events of the past and was now focused on the future.

Jesus said, "All authority in heaven and on earth has been given to me" (28:18, NRSV). He spoke in what we call the divine passive voice, which suggests that the actor is God. God has given him this authority.

This phrase echoes Daniel 7:14: "Rule, glory, and kingship were given to him; all peoples, nations, and languages will serve him. His rule is an everlasting one—it will never pass away!—his kingship is indestructible." Jesus had already referred to the authority that was given to him to forgive sins (Matthew 9:6) and made the claim that "my Father has handed all things over to me" (11:27).

But Jesus' words in Matthew 28:18 take on even greater significance in that he is now the resurrected Jesus, the one who has been victorious over death. He has inaugurated the new order and will be exalted at God's right hand.

Satan offered Jesus "all the kingdoms of the world and their glory" during the temptation (4:8). But now, Jesus, through his obedience to his Father's will, has received far more than Satan offered.

The resurrected Jesus fully embodied the kingship which was introduced in Matthew's royal genealogy (1:1-17), alluded to when the magi searched for the "king of the Jews" (2:2), and enacted in his ride into Jerusalem (21:1-11). Though his kingship had been the subject of mockery (27:11, 29, 37, 42), it was now revealed to be true.

Because Jesus had been given all authority, he could give the Great Commission to his 11 disciples in the next verses. They would have confidence because of his authority.

Verse 19. Jesus linked his authority to the Great Commission with the word "therefore." Because he had received authority, he sent his disciples out with a mission.

As the one with the authority of a king, Jesus had chosen 11 men to be the agents of the inbreaking of his new kingdom. But they were not to be his 11 princes, each assigned a fiefdom. Rather, they were to go out immediately and make more divinely commissioned agents "of all nations" (Matthew 28:19).

Jesus gave them one main imperative from which the rest of the commission flows: to "go and make disciples" (verse 19). Notice how the two verbs "go" and "make" connote proactivity. The commission requires that someone goes and makes disciples.

Why did Jesus say go? The limitation of the gospel to Israel (10:5; 15:24) has now been removed. The message must go to all nations to fully include the Gentiles (28:19). This did not exclude Jews, but it is the Jewish Messiah who completes the salvific work for the whole world.

Why did Jesus say make disciples? The Great Commission is expressed not in terms of its means, but of its end: to make disciples. It is not enough that the nations hear about Jesus. They must also respond as his disciples did, with whole-hearted commitment.

A disciple is a learner or a pupil. Discipleship necessarily begins with the initial proclamation of the gospel but also includes the more arduous task of nurturing the discipleship so the disciple will know everything that Jesus has commanded (verse 20).

The main verb ("make" disciples) is followed by two participles: "baptizing" (verse 19) and "teaching" (verse 20). It is by these two means that disciples are to be made.

Baptizing. Matthew is the only Gospel writer to record Jesus' command to baptize. And the only baptism Matthew has referenced is Jesus' baptism by John (Chapter 3 and referenced in 21:25). But we know that the early church was practicing baptism as a Christian initiation rite (Acts 2:38, 41; 8:12, 38; 9:18; for example). Matthew presumed that his readers were already familiar with Christian baptism.

Note that the baptism of Jesus was in the name of Father, Son, and Holy Spirit. The doctrine of threefold trinitarianism was still in its infancy when this Gospel was written. Some scholars are of the opinion that a later editor added the Trinity to Matthew's original manuscript. But others point to trinitarian language in the letters of Paul that were probably written before Matthew.

Verse 20. *Teaching*. Jesus gave two imperatives to disciple-making: baptizing and teaching. He intended the two to go hand-in-hand.

Though we have no record of Jesus baptizing anyone, he was obviously a teacher and often referred to as such. In Matthew 5:19, Jesus had already mentioned the importance of teaching: "Whoever keeps these commands and teaches people to keep them will be called great in the kingdom of heaven."

Note how Jesus also tied together teaching and compliance. The teaching is "to *obey*" (verse 20; italics added). This is not education for education's sake. Jesus wanted his disciples to pass on a way of living in a manner pleasing to God. In his own teaching, he often emphasized not just learning the letter of the Law, but also the things that arise from adherence to the spirit of the Law.

We see that Jesus also expected his disciples to learn "*everything*" or "*all* that I have commanded you" (Matthew 28:20, RSV; italics added). He spoke of his teaching as a unified whole, not a collection of life lessons from which we can pick and choose.

The final sentence of Matthew's Gospel and the last words he recorded from Jesus are a future-oriented promise. Translators have different ways of starting this sentence. The Greek word literally means "look" (verse 20, CEB). But this is also a special character Matthew has used before to add emphasis. So translations vary from "remember" (NRSV) to "surely" (NIV).

In any case, the promise is the same: "I myself will be with you." The verb is in the present tense, and there is a connotation of ongoing certainty to it: "I am with you *always*" (verse 20, NRSV; italics added). It is not strictly in the future tense. Jesus is and will be with his followers.

Disciples will not be left to serve God as well as they can given what they have learned. Jesus will be an ongoing companion. Those who receive his messengers will receive Jesus himself (Matthew 10:40). In John's Gospel, Jesus says he will send an Advocate to remind the disciples of all that he has commanded them (John 14:26).

But the promise is not entirely open-ended. Time is oriented toward a particular end: "the end of this present age" (Matthew 28:20). In Matthew, we read that the end of the age is to come after the nations hear the good news of the kingdom (24:14) and are prepared for judgment (25:32-36).

The ones to whom Jesus was first speaking did not live to see the end of the present age. They made disciples who made disciples who made disciples and so on, down to our generation. Jesus expects the process to continue. In this way, he will "be with you every day until the end of this present age" (28:20).

Reflect

This is the last lesson of this unit and quarter. The focus of this unit has been "Show and Tell."

We have considered Old and New Testament passages that reveal how we are graced with the opportunity to participate in God's work in the world.

Remember that this is no small matter! The God who created the heavens and the earth has seen fit to include us, creatures that we are, in the cosmic work of building God's kingdom. We take this for granted. God is under no compulsion to include us, yet God has done so, continues to do so, and has promised that it shall be so until "the end of this present age" (Matthew 28:20).

Since the scope of God's work (in which we participate) is cosmic, we have studied some of the central passages of the Bible in this unit. For example, we have read the *Shema* and the Greatest Commandments (Lesson 10). And today, we come to the ultimate directive Jesus gives his disciples: the Great Commission.

As teacher, you will want to impress upon your students the centrality of the Great Commission. Consider giving them this brief review of the preceding lessons in this unit and explaining that the Great Commission is Jesus' "one thing" for us when it comes to Christian mission.

Of all the commissions Jesus has given (see "Connect"), this one is the greatest. It is the most important. If we do nothing else with what Jesus has taught and given us, we should follow the Great Commission. We should make disciples of Jesus Christ!

The stated mission of The United Methodist Church is to "make disciples of Jesus Christ for the transformation of the world." This disciple-making comes in many forms. It can mean first-time conversions, the ongoing process of Christian formation in current disciples, or any combination of those two things. But the one mission of the church is to make disciples of Jesus Christ. Furthermore, it is the mission of every disciple of Jesus to make disciples.

After beginning with a reminder about the scope of this unit, show the segment of the *Adult Bible Studies* DVD related to this lesson if you have it. Then move toward a reading of the Focal Passage.

Consider reading Matthew 28 with this word of introduction: ***Matthew situated today's text on the heels of Jesus' resurrection. The disciples had just experienced the death of the Messiah. Now they will receive from two Marys the word of Jesus' miraculous resurrection. When Jesus met his disciples on an unnamed mountain, he told them to "go and make disciples" (Matthew 28:19).***

Though Matthew did not tell of Jesus' ascension, this text is still upward-looking. For we read about a Jesus who was going to be with the Father in glory so that he can be with the disciples "until the end of this present age" (verse 20). From his vantage point, Jesus wanted to see his disciples make more disciples. He expected them (and us) to continue the disciple-making process he showed us when he called people to follow him and taught them about the kingdom of God.

So Jesus told them directly, "Go and make disciples of all nations, baptizing them in the name of the Father and of the Son and of the Holy Spirit, teaching them to obey everything that I've commanded you" (verses 19-20). Though he had given them various other imperatives in his teaching, this is what he chose to tell them in his risen form, before his departure.

Ask: *If you give someone a list of instructions, what are they most likely to remember?* (*The last instruction.*) *Why do you believe Jesus chose to make his last instruction about disciple-making?*

It is possible, even likely, that a discussion will arise here or at some point about what disciple-making looks like. Some in your class might have equated disciple-making strictly with images of street evangelism, exhorting random passersby to "get right with God."

Point out that disciple-making is more nuanced. Have in mind examples of everyday disciple-making such as spending time with a young person, writing a card of encouragement and including a Bible verse, or praying with a friend. There are many ways to make disciples of Jesus.

The important thing is to be about the task of disciple-making for Jesus. This is not an add-on to the Christian life. We are not to wait for some elusive moment when we've become a perfect Christian and only then begin to think about disciple-making. Our lives are to be a witness, a proclamation, that Jesus Christ is Lord.

In fact, our whole church should be focused on making disciples. As Gary Thompson points out at the beginning of this lesson in the student book, so much of our local church time, money, and resources are focused on institutional maintenance rather than on the mission of disciple-making.

Ask: *What holds you back from being a disciple-maker for Jesus? What holds our church back from being a disciple-making center for Jesus?*

Acknowledge that many Christians today say they feel unprepared by the church to make disciples of Jesus. They feel inadequate and unequal to the task. While we certainly could always improve Christian education and formation, it is natural to feel inadequate to this task. In fact, I would feel concerned if someone told me they felt completely adequate to the task!

Stress that it is the power of the Lord Jesus that is the true power behind disciple-making. He is the one a Christian follows. We Christians are merely signs who point the way to Jesus. And Jesus does not need us to add our own power to the process of making disciples. If we look back over the world history of Christian evangelism, some of our great missteps have occurred when we have added our own power (coercion, intimidation) to Jesus' call.

Since Jesus has given us this Great Commission, challenge class members to envision what it would be like to follow this instruction here and now.

First, remind them of Jesus' promise to be with us "every day until the end of this present age" (verse 20). Also, stress that the call ultimately comes from Jesus. It does not originate in you or me.

Second, note the two things Jesus says for us to do: baptize and teach. These two go together. Those who are baptized are to be taught "everything that I've commanded you" (verse 19). And yet it is Jesus' teaching that often draws people to follow him and be baptized in his name.

Affirm that since it is Jesus' message we share (not our own) and since the power of the gospel comes from Jesus (not from ourselves), we can follow his call to be disciple-makers. His Great Commission can be the mission statement of our lives.

Consider concluding the class with a call to further dedication and action by asking: *How will you live differently this coming week remembering that Jesus has given you the ultimate mission to make disciples for him?*

Remind class members that we invite people to partnership with the potential of leading us to more meaningful discipleship. By participating in Christ's ministry, we not only show our love for God, we reach out to those who we would formally regard as strangers and even enemies.

Close by praying together the prayer at the end of the lesson in the student book: **Dear God, give us your gift of wisdom to help us overcome our lack of understanding. Give us your gift of peace to help us overcome our chaotic lives. Give us your gift of faith to help us overcome our doubts. Give us your gift of courage to help us overcome the fear that hinders us from loving others and sharing your love that can transform lives and change the world; in Jesus' name we pray. Amen.**

[1] From *City Slickers*, written by Lowell Ganz and Babaloo Mandel (Columbia Pictures, 1991) (*imdb.com/title/tt0101587/characters/nm0001588*).

More About Disciple-Making

When we study The Great Commission in Lesson 13, we learn that the mission of the disciples of Jesus Christ is to make more disciples. This is spelled out in Matthew 28:19-20, in which Jesus says, "Therefore, go and make disciples of all nations, baptizing them in the name of the Father and of the Son and of the Holy Spirit, teaching them to obey everything that I've commanded you."

In the student book and teacher book lessons, we try to break down what it means to make disciples. First, we must put aside stereotypes. Street evangelism is just one form of disciple-making to which few people are called. Most disciple-making is relational and takes time, sometimes a great deal of time. It is built on trust.

We also read that Jesus gave us two ways in which he expects disciple-making to take place: baptizing and teaching (Matthew 28:19, 20). As United Methodists, we know that disciple-making for Jesus is the mission of The United Methodist Church.

While I do not wish to alienate any readers who are not United Methodist, I do find that our *Book of Discipline*'s expansion on that mission statement can be informative for Christians of all denominations.

Specifically, the *Discipline* states, "The process for carrying our our mission" means that we:

- proclaim the gospel, seek, welcome and gather persons into the body of Christ;
- lead persons to commit their lives to God through baptism by water and the spirit and profession of faith in Jesus Christ;
- nurture persons in Christian living through worship, the sacraments, spiritual disciplines, and other means of grace, such as Wesley's Christian conferencing;
- send persons into the world to live lovingly and justly as servants of Christ by healing the sick, feeding the hungry, caring for the stranger, freeing the oppressed, being and becoming a compassionate, caring presence, and working to develop social structures that are consistent with the gospel; and
- continue the mission of seeking, welcoming and gathering persons into the community of the body of Christ.[1]

That is about as clear and succinct a way as I think anyone can put it. Perhaps you and your class will want to print those processes out on a page and put them on your classroom wall and tuck them into your Bibles as reminders. When anyone says, "What does it mean to make disciples?" you will have it all right there.

All of those processes require God's grace! They are more than we can do on our own, but God has led us in them for generations. You are evidence of that, disciple!

[1] *The Book Of Discipline of The United Methodist Church, 2016*; page 94.

Coming Next Quarter

Follow

This spring, our lessons center on the theme "Follow." The writer of the student book lessons is Rita Hays; the teacher book writer is David Mosser. Our lessons fall within two units this quarter instead of three so we can mark the six weeks of Lent leading up to Easter.

The Mark You Make

Discipleship in Mark's Gospel is often described as the way of the cross because of the repeated emphasis upon following Jesus on the way to Jerusalem and the command to take up one's cross and follow Jesus (Mark 8:34). In these weeks in which we commemorate Jesus' journey to Jerusalem, we give our attention to various aspects of discipleship highlighted in Mark's Gospel.

We begin with a lesson that helps us better understand Jesus' identity and follow that with lessons on recognizing fellow disciples along the way, understanding Jesus' upside-down kingdom, deepening our understanding of the relationship between faith and prayer, watching for signs of new creation breaking through, and accepting Jesus' forgiveness when we as his disciples miss the mark. We conclude this unit with a celebration of Jesus' resurrection based on Mark's account of the empty tomb.

The Steps You Take

Creation care has become a prominent topic of discussion in Christian congregations and seminaries during the last couple of decades. While there is disagreement about human responsibility for climate change and to what extent we should limit human activity for the purpose of preservation of endangered species and habitats, Scripture makes clear that God takes pleasure in creation and that our role as stewards requires that we appreciate creation and take our responsibility as stewards seriously.

The lessons in this unit lead us to better observe God's beautiful creation, understand why all of God's creation needs sabbath, grow in our understanding of tithing as stewardship of God's resources, acknowledge the limits of our understanding when confronted with the complexities of creation, anticipate God's restoration of creation, and model God's generosity by paying it forward.

CPSIA information can be obtained
at www.ICGtesting.com
Printed in the USA
BVHW010610200122
626624BV00016B/2175